TWAYNE'S WORLD AUTHORS SERIES

A Survey of the World's Literature

Sylvia E. Bowman, Indiana University

GENERAL EDITOR

THE NETHERLANDS

Egbert Krispyn, University of Georgia

EDITOR

Desiderius Erasmus

TWAS 353

IMAGO · ERASMI · ROTERODA
MI · AB · ALBERTO · DVRERO · AD
VIVAM · EFFIGIEM · DELINIATA ·

ΤΗΝ · ΚΡΕΙΤΤΩ · ΤΑ · ΣΥΓΓΡΑΜ
ΜΑΤΑ · ΔΕΙΞΕΙ

· M · D · X X V I ·

Desiderius Erasmus

Desiderius Erasmus

J. KELLEY SOWARDS

Wichita State University

TWAYNE PUBLISHERS

A DIVISION OF G. K. HALL & CO., BOSTON

Library of Congress Cataloging in Publication Data

Sowards, Jesse Kelley, 1924–
  Desiderius Erasmus.

  (Twayne's world authors series; TWAS 353: The
Netherlands)
  Bibliography: p. 143–46.
  Includes index.
  1. Erasmus, Desiderius, d. 1536.

B785.E64S68   199′.492   74–23864

ISBN 0–8057–2302–1

To Steve, Elizabeth, and Mike

Contents

About the Author

J. Kelley Sowards is Endowment Association Distinguished Professor in Humanities and Professor of History at Wichita State University. He was formerly Dean of the Fairmount College of Liberal Arts and Sciences at Wichita State University. He has edited (with Paul Pascal) *The Julius exclusus of Erasmus* (London and Bloomington: Indiana University Press, 1968). His other works on Erasmus include the monographs *Erasmus and the "Other" Pope Julius, Erasmus and the Making of Julius exclusus,* and *Erasmus in England,* in the Wichita State University "University Studies" series, as well as articles on Erasmus in *Studies in Philology, Studies in the Renaissance,* and *Moreana.* Professor Sowards is one of the editors of *The Collected Works of Erasmus,* being published by the University of Toronto Press. He is also the author of *Western Civilization to 1660* (New York: St. Martin's Press, 1964) and editor/author of *The Eve of the Modern World* in *Critical Issues in History,* 2 vols. (Boston: D. C. Heath, 1967). His two-volume *Makers of the Western Tradition* will be published by St. Martin's Press in 1975.

Foreword

Desiderius Erasmus of Rotterdam was the most famous man of letters of the early sixteenth century, a figure who dominated the intellectual world of his time as clearly as Petrarch, Voltaire, or Goethe did theirs. Yet to modern readers, even fairly sophisticated ones, he is almost unknown. They may recall that he had some vague connection with the Reformation or with Martin Luther but usually will not know "what side" he was on. Or they may know that he wrote the *Praise of Folly*, though few these days will have read it. Even fewer will be aware that, beyond this one famous book, the titles of his other works run into the hundreds, his letters into the thousands.

The intention of this book is to present to modern readers a brief survey of Erasmus as a man of letters. It does not pretend to be a comprehensive biography in either form or content: several good ones already exist. It is rather a literary study. Attention is paid mainly to his writings but also to the events of both Erasmus's own life and the larger world, as those events affected his writings. Determining which events influenced his writing, however, is not an easy thing, for his life and times were interwoven with his writings. He was a man of letters, and his response to the events of his life and times was invariably a literary response. Thus the reader must be prepared to be drawn back repeatedly from a concern with his works to be reminded of the events that shaped a particular piece of writing.

The book is organized in a series of chapters dealing with the several categories of Erasmus's writings—his satirical works, devotional works, works of scholarship, controversial writings, and writings against war. But it is also strung on a chronology in order to ease the task of relating his works to the historical events that formed them.

From his own time to the present, Erasmus has always tended to be a protean figure to those interested in him or in the age of the Reformation, in which he played so prominent a role. He has been seen as Erasmus "the heretic" who "laid the egg that Luther hatched." He has been seen as "the Protestant Erasmus," the enemy of all that was bad in the old church and whose criticism was instrumental in pulling it down. He has been seen as Erasmus the *philosophe*, the rationalist born out of time and doomed to live uncomfortably in an irrational age. He has been Erasmus the liberal, Erasmus the conservative, Erasmus the moral coward, and Erasmus the apostle of toleration. He was likely all these things to some extent, and more. But this book will not take a special point of view on Erasmus nor venture so ambitious a task as a new interpretation of him. The reader may draw his own conclusions and interpret him as he likes.

But if the author may suggest an inference, it may be instructive for our time—a time that has been called "the age of permanent crisis"—to study for a moment a man who was caught in the crisis of another age, the crushing crisis of the Reformation, and who insisted upon holding to his own view of what was important to his world, who insisted upon thinking and speaking "otherwise," and who resisted the simplistic demand that crisis always makes, that one must be either "for us or against us."

Acknowledgments

I wish to thank the following publishers for their kind permission to use excerpts from the items indicated: the New American Library for passages from *The Essential Erasmus*, John P. Dolan, ed. and trans. (1964); University of Chicago Press for quotations from *The Colloquies of Erasmus*, Craig R. Thompson, ed. and trans. (1965); Cambridge University Press for passages from Margaret Mann Phillips, *The "Adages" of Erasmus* (1964); Frederick Ungar Publishing Co. for passages from *Erasmus-Luther Discourse on Free Will*, Ernst F. Winter, ed. and trans. (1961); Harper & Row for passages from Desiderius Erasmus, *Christian Humanism and the Reformation*, John C. Olin, ed. (1965) and *Erasmus and his Age, Selected Letters of Desiderius Erasmus*, Hans J. Hillerbrand, ed. (1970); Indiana University Press for quotations from *The Enchiridion of Erasmus*, Raymond Himelick, trans. and ed. (1963), and *The Julius exclusus of Erasmus*, J. Kelley Sowards, ed., Paul Pascal, trans. (1968); and Hendricks House, for excerpts from *The Praise of Folly by Desiderius Erasmus*, Leonard F. Dean, trans. and ed. (1946).

I am also grateful to the Rijksmuseum, Amsterdam, for permission to reproduce the Dürer engraving of Erasmus for the frontispiece.

I wish to thank the Wichita State University Research Committee, its chairman, Dean Lloyd M. Benningfield, and Mr. Frederick Sudermann, Director of Research and Sponsored Programs, for generous financial assistance in the preparation of the manuscript, and Mrs. Margaret Shapley for typing the final version of it.

Chronology

1467   Probable date of Erasmus's birth.

1476   To school at Deventer, influence of the Brethren of the Common Life.

1480–   Death of both parents, victims of the plague.
1481

1487   Enters the monastery of the Augustinian Canons at Steyn.

1492   Ordained priest, leaves the monastery as Latin secretary to the Bishop of Cambrai.

1495   Theological student, University of Paris.

1499   First visit to England.

1500–   At Paris and in Low Countries, studies Greek.
1505

1500   Publication of first edition of *Adagia*.

1503   Publication of *Enchiridion Militis Christiani*.

1506   Second visit to England and departure for Italy.

1506   Receives doctor's degree, University of Torino.

1508   Aldine edition of *Adagia* published (Venice).

1509   Visits Rome and returns to England.

1509–   In England, London and Cambridge.
1514

1512   Publication of *Praise of Folly*.

1513   *Julius exclusus* probably written.

1516   Publication of the Greek New Testament and the works of St. Jerome by the Froben press (Basel).

1517   Publication of *The Complaint of Peace*.

1517   Outbreak of the Lutheran Reformation.

1519   Publication of the first edition of the *Colloquies*.

1520   Pope Leo X's bull against Luther, *Exsurge Domine*.

1521   Luther's condemnation at the Diet of Worms.

1521–   Erasmus in Basel.
1529

1524   *On Free Will*, Erasmus's book against Luther.

1528   Publication of *Ciceronianus*.

1529   Erasmus driven from Basel by the tumult of the Reformation there.

1529–   Residence in Freiburg in Breisgau.
1535

1536   Death of Erasmus in Basel.

CHAPTER 1

The Hearth, the Cloister, and the World: The Youth of Erasmus

OUR best authority on Erasmus is Erasmus himself. Despite a lifetime of frail health and chronic illnesses, bitter and exhausting controversies and relentless labor of the most demanding sort—and somewhat to his own surprise—he lived to old age and to see himself celebrated as the most famous literary figure of his time.

Throughout his long life he was a tireless letter writer. In spite of the attrition of time his surviving letters number more than three thousand and fill eleven heavy volumes.[1] In 1523 he wryly commented to a friend, "I have written and continue to write so many letters that two wagons would scarcely suffice to carry them."[2] From an early time he kept careful copies of his letters and, starting with the edition of 1515, he steadily published and reissued collections of his *epistolae* that were among his most popular and widely circulated books. For long stretches of time the letters constitute virtually a day to day chronicle of his life, containing reports on his health, his diet, his travels; his hopes, fears, suspicions, and aspirations; his troubles with a balky horse, a thieving deliveryman, an overzealous customs official, or a forgetful patron; waspish comments on his publishers and his critics; graceful dedications of classical translations and critical editions of the ancients and the church fathers addressed to popes, cardinals, bishops, kings, councillors and courtiers, and to friends of every class and station.

His books, like his letters, are rich in biographical detail. There are hundreds of them, including dozens of revisions and enlargements of major works and single editions and combinations of smaller and minor works in various editions. Just as many of Erasmus's letters are actually tracts and pamphlets of considerable length, many of his books are as short and personal as letters. This is particularly

1

true of the almost endless stream of *apologiae*, attacks upon his critics and detractors, and defences of his work that grew out of the literary and religious controversies in which he was involved for most
of his mature life.

Both these controversies and the fame of Erasmus as he grew older
inspired friends and admirers to request of him an authentic auto-
biography, particularly one that would throw light on his early years,
before he had gained the stature of "The Prince of Humanists." In
response, Erasmus did write several such accounts, but always with
extreme reluctance, usually in haste, and almost always vague and
incomplete. The most important of these he called *Compendium Vitae Erasmi Roterodami*. It was written from Basel in the early spring
of 1524 and addressed to Conrad Goclen, a young professor of Latin
at the Collegium Trilingue in Louvain, and one of Erasmus's two
or three most trusted friends at that time. But even this account was
brief to the point of abruptness—it runs to only six pages in the
standard printed edition. The title Erasmus scribbled above the text
means "short sketch"; he subtitled it, in Greek, "The Secret Life"
and swore Goclen to the most "profound silence . . . so that you
must not trust my secret even to your most intimate friend."[3]

What had finally brought Erasmus to this distasteful task was the
precarious state of his health. The winter of 1524 in Basel had been
unusually harsh and Erasmus had suffered so severely from his
chronic attacks of kidney stone that he was sure he would not live
beyond Christmas. As he slowly recovered in the spring, the sobering
recollection of his attacks, his general frailty, and the imminence of
old age—he was then in his middle fifties—all combined to make
him aware that he must set down those facts of his life he wanted
posterity to know and for which friends like Goclen had been clam-
oring. The task was no more appealing to him for all that, and he
undertook it glumly and with his usual haste: the first entries are
short, abrupt fragments, notes rather than narrative, "Born at Rotterdam on the vigil of Simon and Jude. Numbers about fifty-seven
years."[4]

This seeming uncertainty about his precise age, so curious at first
glance, is in large part the reason for Erasmus's reluctance to set
down the facts of his early life. For he had been an illegitimate child.
This unhappy fact was, moreover, the beginning of the "Iliad of
woes"[5] that made up his early years, so painful to recall even from
the pinnacle of his fame and across so many years.

I *Early Years*

Erasmus's reluctance about his early life and his evasiveness about his age had less to do with the fact of his illegitimacy than with the complicating circumstances surrounding it. For he was not only illegitimate, he was the illegitimate son of a priest. Despite the story he finally tells in the *Compendium Vitae* of a "star-crossed" romance and a tragic pair of young lovers, the truth seems to have been a much more sordid and much more ordinary matter—that of a young priest living with a village girl in a continuing liaison over a number of years and fathering not only Erasmus but another son some three years older. The town was Gouda and the year of Erasmus's birth most likely 1467.[6]

It is probably true, as Erasmus tells us, that his father, Gerard, had some learning, had traveled and studied in Italy, and "provided a liberal education for his boy and sent him to school when scarcely more than four years old,"[7] probably the village grammar school of Gouda. But then, "in his ninth year," his father sent him to the Cathedral School of St. Lebwin's in Deventer. Despite Erasmus's later contemptuous recollection of it, this was one of the best lower schools in the Netherlands. It was connected with the great lay religious order of the Brethren of the Common Life, one of whose most important centers was Deventer and who were as famed for their schools as for their piety. Both the training he received at the hands of the Brethren and the religious impressions to which he was so early exposed were to be profoundly influential upon Erasmus.[8]

Equally influential was to be another movement beginning even to affect the pious Brethren schools of Erasmus's youth and indeed much of the culture of northern Europe—that of Renaissance Humanism. Already for more than a century Italian bankers and businessmen, diplomats, clerics, and scholars had carried the New Learning of Italy to the north, with their elegantly contrived Latin style, their adoration of the pagan classics, and often a knowledge of Greek. By the same token, bright young men from England, France, Germany, Bohemia, the Low Countries had flocked to Italy to study and learn, like Erasmus's father Gerard. They returned to their homelands filled with their zeal for Humanism and ready to spread its influence. And that influence touched the young Deventer schoolboy.

Erasmus did not complete the course at Deventer, for, when he had reached the third class, "a plague which at that time raged in

the town, carried off his mother. . . . When the sickness became
worse and worse every day, so that the whole house where he lived
was ravaged by it" he and his brother were sent back to Gouda where
shortly their father also died of the pestilence. Erasmus was thirteen
or fourteen at this time and, he tells us, his parents barely forty.[9] The
guardians appointed to care for the sons and administer their meager estate sent them to another school of the Brethren, this time at
's-Hertogenbosch. Erasmus continued to be a good student as he had
been at Deventer. The school master of 's-Hertogenbosch, a man
named Rombold, "was much pleased with the capacity of the boy,"
Erasmus tells us, and "began to solicit him to become one of his
flock."[10] And it is indeed likely that this would have happened and
that the bright, bookish boy, already singled out by his teachers,
would have completed his training and followed their path. But
the plague continued to rage. One of his guardians died of it and
Erasmus himself was stricken for more than a year. Famine and war
followed pestilence as Holland was caught up in the convulsion of
the Burgundian states following the death of the great Duke Charles
the Bold at Nancy (1477). The small inheritance of Erasmus and his
brother rapidly disappeared. In the face of these circumstances, in
such perilous times, their substance gone, and no security to be had,
the remaining guardians resolved to place the boys in a monastery.

In later years there was no more bitter recollection for Erasmus
than this decision. He charged his guardians with treachery and
mismanagement of the estate. He accused the school authorities of
collusion with the guardians and of making "a regular business of
hunting up boys to be trained . . . for the monastic life."[11] The
guardians, meanwhile, had found a place for their charges, and a
very good place, at the monastery of Sion near Delft, the principal
house of the regional chapter of the Augustinian Canons Regular.
The brother Peter accepted and Erasmus raged against him for his
betrayal and continued to hold out, insisting that he deserved to go
to the university. Then one day, as Erasmus tells the story, ". . . by
mere chance he was making a visit to one [of the houses] of the same
order at Emmaus or Stein, near Gouda. There he fell in with Cornelius, formerly his chamber-fellow at Deventer, who had not yet put
on the religious habit; he had seen Italy, but had come back without
having learnt much. This young man, for a purpose of his own,
began to depict with marvelous fluency that holy sort of life, the
abundance of books, the ease, the quiet, the angelic companionship,

and what not? A childish affection drew Erasmus towards his old schoolfellow. Some friends enticed and some pushed him on. The fever weighed upon him. He chose this spot, having no taste for the other."[12] The year was probably 1487, and Erasmus was nineteen or twenty years old.

II   *The Monk in Cloister*

In this way Erasmus entered the monastery of the Augustinian Canons at Steyn: we have no reason to question the general outline of the story. Despite his later charges of perfidy against his guardians, treachery on the part of his brother, the collusion of his schoolmasters, and the inference that for some sinister "purpose of his own" his friend Cornelius and others lured him on, there was in fact no good alternative to the decision. Where was another career open to such a boy outside the church, without trade, profession, influence, or substance? It is clear, moreover, that it was not the "holy sort of life" nor the ease nor the quiet promised by the monastery that finally induced the young Erasmus to enter Steyn but "the abundance of books" that Cornelius spoke of.

The novitiate year passed and Erasmus recalled that he ". . . was cheered by the pleasant companionship of the younger inmates of the convent; songs were sung, games were played, verses were capped, he was not compelled to fast, nor roused from his bed for the nightly services. No one found fault, no one scolded; all were kind and cheerful."[13] He had books, leisure, and friends: and there is no reason to believe that the taking of his final vows either radically changed the pattern of his life or marked so desperate a crisis as he later claimed. There is no hint of crisis, indeed no mention at all of his vows in the correspondence that is preserved from the years at Steyn. Rather the letters continue to reflect the company of good and congenial friends and a life of books and study—the very attractions that had finally lured Erasmus inside the walls of the monastery.

Some of these letters show him as the preceptor of his friends, encouraging their study of the classics and revealing his own growing erudition. To Cornelius, who had followed Erasmus into orders and who resided at a nearby convent, he wrote, "I have my guides whom I follow; if you perhaps have others, I shall not take it amiss. My authorities in Poetry are Maro, Horace, Naso, Juvenal, Statius,

Martial, Claudian, Persius, Lucan, Tibullus and Propertius; in prose, Tully, Quintilian, Sallust, Terence. Then, for the observation of elegances, there is no one in whom I have so much confidence as Laurentius Valla, who is unrivalled both in the sharpness of his intelligence and the tenacity of his memory."[14] In another early letter to Cornelius he continued the list of his modern authorities, again none more praised than Valla—"where do you find more observance of ancient elegance"—"or Philelphus, where more eloquence than in Aeneas Silvius, Augustinus Dathus, Guarino, Poggio or Gasperino." Not only does he cite this familiar list of Italian humanists but northerners such as the great Rudolph Agricola, his own schoolmaster at Deventer Alexander Hegius, and (perhaps with a sly smile) their mutual friend, his young fellow monk and aspiring poet, Willem Hermans of Gouda.[15] Beatus Rhenanus, his later friend and biographer, tells us that "as a boy Erasmus knew the comedies of Terence as familiarly as his own fingers"[16] and "Horace by heart."[17]

But, at the same time, he was equally familiar with the Christian classics. In another note to Cornelius he writes of the letters of St. Jerome, "I have not only read them long ago, but have written every one of them out with my own fingers,"[18] the beginning surely of the great editorial project of his later years.

Others letters are clearly epistolary exercises. One series of them is addressed to his friend and fellow monk Servatius Rogerus, exemplifying the turgid, florid type of the "letter of endearment."[19] He exchanged literary pieces with Willem Hermans and a fine mock heroic contest ensued. Cornelius writes that he has added some verses of his own to a poem of Erasmus's *On the Contempt of Poetry*, converting it into a dialogue. And, in the same letter, he asks for Erasmus's criticisms of a tract of his *De Morte*. Probably of this type of exercise was Erasmus's own substantial tract *De Contemptu Mundi*, almost surely written about this time as an example of the classical *suasoria* ("rhetorical persuasion"). Many years later he was to be embarrassed by its publication and by the implication that he held the opinions he expressed so persuasively.[20] He wrote orations in the classical style and on several of the topics conventional for this literary form, including a little *Oration on Peace and Discord*.

Thus in these years at Steyn we find Erasmus studying, reading, constantly practicing every kind of literary form, driven always by what he called a "secret natural impulse . . . to good literature,"[21] but equally driven by his passion to master the tools of the New

Learning. For he had chosen literature as his way of advancement, his way to become a person of importance, to rise above his origins, to gain fame, position, and independence.

But neither fame, position, nor certainly independence was really possible for a cloistered monk. In spite of the good will and indulgence of his superiors—and there is every reason to believe they were indulgent with the young Erasmus—the limitations of the monastery pressed increasingly upon him. To his embarrassment, the literary ardor of the letters to his friend Servatius had been misinterpreted either by Servatius himself or by their superiors and either or both of the young monks were rebuked. There were, probably from the beginning, some brothers who disapproved of Erasmus's devotion to literature and study or perhaps were resentful of privileges the young scholar received. How general such antagonism was we do not know, but "the weapons . . . of jealousy and abuse" stung nevertheless.[22] His superiors may have restricted his studies in some ways: perhaps even prohibiting them for a while. Here was a jolting reminder that his life was not his own, that even his beloved books could be taken from him. He resentfully turned to the planning of a book "to avenge myself with my pen."[23] It was to be called *Antibarbarorum Liber*, *The Book against the Barbarians*. And, although it is difficult to say how much of the work was actually completed at this time, the bundle of themes it contained clearly anticipate the preoccupations of Erasmus's mature years. The "barbarians" of the title were, of course, most immediately his fellow monks and his insensitive superiors. Thus we see the beginning of Erasmus's disenchantment with monasticism that was to ripen into the bitterest hatred of his later life. But he included in his indictment not only the monastic orders but all those so-called religious who ignored or, worse, rejected the study of literature, the cultivation of style and learning, and especially the great tradition of classical culture. He argued that the classical tradition at its best was not alien to the Christian life but a necessary base for it.

He argued further that the greatest minds of the church—the learned fathers Jerome, Augustine, Chrysostom, and Basil did not reject the classical tradition but embraced it. In this sort of defence of letters and its corollary argument that learning is essential to the Christian vocation Erasmus was to labor unstintingly the rest of his life, never wavering from his conviction that "good letters make good men."

Even as he worked at this attack upon the barbarism of his fellow monks the opportunity came for him to leave them, to become Latin secretary to the nearby Bishop of Cambrai, Hendrik van Bergen. That this was not a sudden decision nor an angry act of hurt and rebellion is shown by the events surrounding his departure. His superiors seem not only to have permitted but to have encouraged it. Indeed it is likely that they secured his appointment. For it must have been as clear to them as to Erasmus that their brilliant young brother had no real vocation for the monastic life. They may have hoped that his talents would bring honor to their house and their order, and they surely knew that to bring those talents to fruition he needed the experience of the wider world outside the monastery, the world he longed for but really knew only in the pages of his books. On the eve of his departure in the spring of 1492 they saw to it that he was ordained priest, perhaps to give him greater status in his new appointment but surely an act of confidence as they sped him on his way, with their blessings.

III   *The Monk out of Cloister*

The appointment to the bishop's staff was particularly attractive. Not only was he a great and wealthy ecclesiastical lord and one with a reputation for the promotion of learning, but more important, certainly for Erasmus, he was planning to go to Italy, where he expected to be made a cardinal. Indeed, it was probably this matter that had led him to seek the services of the facile young Latin scholar.

The first months passed happily enough at the bishop's court. There was the excitement of new tasks and new surroundings, but most of all, the excitement of anticipating the visit to Italy. Erasmus wrote frequently to his old friends at Steyn and returned to visit occasionally. He met new and stimulating people and his spirit soared.

But it shortly became apparent that the eagerly anticipated journey to Italy would not materialize: the bishop was not to be elevated to the cardinalate. Erasmus was disappointed and restless. He appealed to the bishop to sponsor him for admission to the University of Paris and the bishop complied, promising his support and patronage. It is even probable that he was instrumental in gaining the permission of Erasmus's superiors at Steyn for this new enterprise and continued absence. Here was the opportunity to study for the advanced theological degree that would clearly benefit both Erasmus and his house. Moreover, the bishop was commending the young brother to the reformed College de Montaigu and to the charge of his friend Jan Standonk, the master of the college, who himself had close ties with Steyn and Gouda. Such an arrangement surely allayed any doubts his superiors may have had, and by the late summer of 1495 Erasmus was installed at Montaigu under the watchful eye of Master Jan.

The arrangements may have exactly suited his monastic superiors, but it was hardly what Erasmus had hoped for. The college was ruled with a savage discipline and was so sternly ascetic that Erasmus later claimed many students became sick, some even died from the meager, rotten food and contaminated water.

Within a few months under such conditions Erasmus himself became ill and was forced to return to the household of the bishop, sick at heart, discouraged, and vowing never to return to Paris. He was well received by the bishop and recovered his strength. And again with the encouragement of his superiors at Steyn, he returned to Paris and his studies, though they permitted him this time to take private lodgings rather than return to Montaigu.

But his new freedom was costly and he had no greater resources than before. The bishop's support was minimal and often did not come at all. Erasmus sought other patrons with little greater success. The plague came and went, forcing him almost every year to interrupt his work and return to Holland. Though he disliked the distraction, he took private pupils for tutoring in Latin rhetoric: indeed, it was his principal means to eke out a living. Through it all he continued his studies, though fitfully and without enthusiasm. Even under more favorable circumstances this might easily have been the case. For the great University of Paris, once the intellectual center of Europe, had begun to decline into its most evil days. There was incessant wrangling among the factions and orders and the adherents of the various schools of theology. Theology itself had become hopelessly stilted and mired in irrelevancies. Adding to the confusion was the conflict between traditional scholasticism and the new humanistic studies, which had their advocates at Paris as elsewhere.

Erasmus was, of course, already wholeheartedly committed to these new studies, and, as soon as he reached Paris, he sought out the company of the Parisian humanists. Chief among them was Robert Gaguin, a distinguished scholar, public servant, and churchman and,

like Standonk, a Fleming. But there the resemblance ended, for unlike Standonk, he was both a patron and practitioner of the new
learning and its champion in the university. Erasmus may have had
letters of introduction to Gaguin from friends in the Low Countries.
We know that he sent Gaguin some of his poems and that the master
was greatly impressed by them and extended his valuable friendship
to Erasmus. Erasmus showed him the manuscript of the *Antibarbari*,
and, while it pleased Gaguin well enough, he advised his young
friend against its publication since it might be damaging to his career.
But he did encourage him in another venture, the publication of a
small collection of poems by Erasmus's old friend and fellow monk
Willem Hermans (including one of Erasmus's own and a letter of
dedication to his patron the Bishop of Cambrai), which was printed
in the winter of 1496–97. By the time this book appeared Gaguin
had already given another opportunity to Erasmus to gain some celebrity. In the fall of 1495 Gaguin's history of France, *De Origine
et Gestis Francorum Compendium*, was about to be published. He
invited Erasmus, among others, to contribute a complimentary notice to fill out the last few blank pages of the printed edition. The
resulting graceful letter is Erasmus's first publication, the beginning
of his lifelong love affair with the press.

Gaguin had, moreover, introduced his young protégé into his circle of Parisian humanists, where the grace and elegance of his Latin
style, obvious learning, quick wit, and affability made him quickly
accepted. The group included not only Frenchmen and Netherland-
ers—among them Erasmus's friend Cornelius Gerard and one of
his future printers Josse Bade of Assche—but the turbulent, bawdy,
brawling Italian humanists who had begun to flock to Paris, seeking
employment in and around the university, the city, and the court.
One of these was Fausto Andrelini, a pupil of Filelfo, who had lived
in Paris since about 1490 and taught rhetoric at the university. His
life was something of a scandal and at the very time Erasmus came
to know him he was involved in a noisy and vulgar quarrel with another Italian, Girolamo Balbi, and "volleys of invective" were being
exchanged in the best Italian manner. It was only Andrelini's close-
ness to the court (he was shortly appointed Royal Poet) that prevented public or university authorities from moving against him.
And it was with Andrelini that Erasmus struck up a close friendship
that quickened his life in Paris.

The allurements of his humanistic studies and the heady company of his humanist friends only made his formal studies more unattractive to him. As an older student with considerable previous academic training Erasmus was either routinely dispensed from the lower degree requirements or easily satisfied them and by 1498 was probably a formal candidate for the doctorate in theology—the purpose for which his brothers had sent him to Paris. But by this time he had lost interest in pursuing the work and, probably under the influence of his humanist friends, was dreaming of Italy once more "where the walls are more learned and more eloquent than our men. . . . What we here think eloquent and beautiful cannot but seem poor and rude and tasteless there."[24] Both his own ambition and the expectations of his monastic superiors could be served if he could find a way to take his doctorate at the great University of Bologna. His letters are filled with his plans and hopes and his frustrations as they fail to materialize. The most promising possibility was offered by one of his tutorial pupils, a wealthy young English nobleman, William Blount Lord Mountjoy. But Mountjoy decided not to go. Instead he invited his tutor to accompany him to England and Erasmus accepted. It was the spring of the year 1499.

IV   England and the Wider World

Erasmus spent the summer at Mountjoy's country house in Hartfordshire enjoying an ease and luxury he had never known before. He wrote his friend Andrelini of the hunting parties and the English girls with their angels' faces and delightful propensity to kiss at the slightest provocation. Mountjoy took him to his other residences and to London, where he introduced him to the circle of English men of letters, scholars, humanists, and patrons—the teacher and rhetorician William Grocyn, the humanist physician and Greek scholar Thomas Linacre, the theologian John Colet, and the precocious young Thomas More—the so-called Oxford Reformers who were to be counted among his dearest friends and who were to exert such a powerful influence upon his life. Not the least of these was Thomas More, who, though ten or twelve years Erasmus's junior and still a student in the law courts, was already a young humanist of brilliant promise. The occasion of their first meeting may well have been at Mountjoy's residence near Greenwich. More and another English friend took Erasmus for a walk to "the next village" and without any warning introduced the unsuspecting Dutchman

into the presence of the children of the royal family, staying at El-
tham Palace, and the boy-scholar Prince Henry standing in their
midst. More graciously presented his compliments to Henry with
some writings: Erasmus, the "poet" and visiting celebrity, was not
prepared and could only promise a literary gift at a later time. He
was further flustered shortly to receive a note from Henry asking for
his gift and was forced to retire for three days of hard work com-
posing and polishing a proper poem. But no harm was done: indeed,
the reverse. More had put his new friend in the way of important
patronage and, at the same time, had revealed to him probably the
first instance of that sly, wry humor that was to be an ingredient of
their lifelong friendship.

Within a few weeks Erasmus accepted the invitation of John Colet
to come to Oxford, where Colet was a lecturer in Holy Scripture in
Magdelene College. Like the older Linacre and Grocyn, Colet had
studied in Italy. He had been deeply influenced by the Christian
Neoplatonism of Marsilio Ficino and his school and had returned
to Oxford to develop his own theological ideas, which he had begun
to do in a series of lectures and sermons on the New Testament
already celebrated by the time Erasmus arrived in Oxford. Colet
shared with Erasmus an impatience with scholastic formalism and
the endless, arid speculation that dominated traditional theology at
Oxford as at Paris. Colet had turned instead to the text of the Gospels
and the Pauline letters in an attempt to understand and explain them
in the light of simple, historical Christianity—apart from systems
and subtleties.

Colet, impressed by the learning and drawn by the feeling of
shared purpose he sensed in Erasmus, invited him to prolong his
stay at Oxford and join him, taking up the exposition of the Old
Testament as he was dealing with the New. Erasmus refused the invitation in a long letter to Colet, gracefully but firmly. He was simply
not that interested in the Old Testament and did not yet possess the
scholarly equipment he knew he required for such a task. Other con-
siderations may have weighed in his decision as well. The very inten-
sity of Colet's religious commitment, his puritanical seriousness and
total lack of humor set Erasmus's teeth on edge. Nor were the two
men totally agreed on several aspects of approach and methodology.
There was the fact that he had not apparently bothered to inform his
monastic superiors that he was going or had gone to England. Nevertheless, Colet's intense sense of purpose had profoundly touched

Erasmus and wakened echoes of purpose in him that he had not expressed since his days at Steyn. Colet's challenge had made him realize the direction in which his own haphazard studies had been leading him and, at the same time, had made him starkly aware of the deficiencies and lapses in those studies. He now knew as never before that he must be a theologian—not the kind he had come to despise at Paris and more recently at Oxford, a despite he shared with Colet, but a theologian who would put the revolution of humanist learning to work upon the sacred texts of the Christian tradition. He now knew that his dalliance with poetry, rhetoric, and other secular studies had really been preparation for this more profound study.

But most of all he realized that if he now turned seriously to this study, if he wanted to discover the historical basis of Christianity, he must have Greek. Erasmus had been exposed to it from time to time since his schoolboy days at Deventer but never either seriously or intensively. It was to this deficiency that he referred in his letter to Colet, ironically by quoting in Greek the proverb "to train oneself as a potter by setting to work on an amphora." Colet, who had little or no Greek himself, did not fully share Erasmus's views in this matter. But to Erasmus it was as essential to return to the letter of the Scriptures as to their spirit. For Colet the spirit was enough. At the end of January, 1500, Erasmus left for the continent, for Paris, and for study.

The next few years were the hardest and most desperate of Erasmus's life. He had the goal of his study at last firmly fixed before him; he knew what he had to do. Perhaps for that very reason the poverty and sickness, the frustrations and interruptions that dogged his steps were more intolerable than ever. His patrons were negligent. The Bishop of Cambrai was "not even friendly"[25]—Standonk had given the bishop a bad report on Erasmus's malingering at the university, and he was never able to repair his relations with him. He approached the bishop's brother, Antonius van Bergen, the wealthy Abbot of St. Bertin, in the hope that he could arouse the abbot's generosity with his new program of study. But he was mistaken— "the Abbot bids me be of good cheer!"[26] The generosity of his less exalted patrons and friends was soon exhausted as were their contacts with other possible benefactors. During these first months of his return to Paris he wrote to a friend in the Low Countries,

My Greek studies are almost too much for my courage; while I have not the means of purchasing books, or the help of a teacher. And while I am in all this trouble, I have scarcely the wherewithal to sustain life; so much is our learning worth to us![27]

It was at this desperate time and in these desperate circumstances that he was forced to find out how much indeed his learning was worth to him. He turned to the printing press. He had gained some small reputation from his association with Gaguin's history and from the publication of his and Willem Hermans's poems. He had contacts with printers and booksellers through Gaguin and his other friends in Paris and some such connections leading back to his early years in the Low Countries. He had, moreover, a valuable literary commodity in the facile, elegant, and fashionable Latin style that he had cultivated since boyhood. And he had a dozen projects—some in bits and pieces, some substantially complete, some only in mind. A few still unpublished poems, the manuscript of the *Antibarbari*, and copies of his letters had been circulated among his friends and were admired by them. Other pieces had grown out of his own study and his friends urged him to publish them. These were largely of the type of critical editions of standard classical authors for which the continuing popularity of the classics and the fashion of Humanism created a profitable market. In the course of the year 1500 Erasmus prepared an edition of Cicero's *De Officiis* for the press of Joannes Philippi in Paris. As his hard struggle with Greek progressed and he became able to handle the language with some ease, he turned his exercises and drills to the same sort of profit, preparing translations of Greek authors into Latin. As early as the winter of 1500 he was at work on Plato and had borrowed a Greek Homer from a friend. Within two more years he was working on the translation of three declamations of Libanius and shortly thereafter on the dialogues of the second century Greek satirist Lucian, who was to remain his favorite Greek author. Throughout his life Erasmus was to continue this sort of editorial work, translations of, and commentaries on, the standard classical writers. Of the Latin authors, among others, he would prepare editions of Livy, Pliny, Suetonius, Seneca; of the poets Horace, Ovid, and Persius; and of the dramatists Plautus and Terence. Of the Greek writers he would do Latin translations of Euripides, Plutarch, and of course more of the dialogues of Lucian, and prepare editions of Aesop, Demosthenes, Galen, Xenophon, and even Aristotle. These books, often published in small segments so that work on one author could produce several individual titles, which could be recombined into new editions and republished, some of them several times, contributed to making Erasmus one of the most prolific writers of his age; and his never failing mastery of style, the insight and trenchancy of his commentaries and notes, and the felicity of his translations made him one of the most popular as well. And he had, in these as in his several other kinds of writings, a shrewd eye for the book market. Probably excepting only Martin Luther, Erasmus was to become the most widely read and widely bought author of his generation.

In those hard-pressed years at the turn of the sixteenth century Erasmus often complained of how these secular occupations got in the way of his work in Greek and his more serious interests: if only he could be free of them, "I should then devote myself entirely to the study of Sacred Literature, as for some time I have longed to do."[28] Despite such protests—and they were always a little rhetorical— these secular occupations were part and parcel of his more serious interests. For the reputation of Erasmus the classical humanist be- came the foundation for Erasmus the Christian scholar and tended to lend authority to whatever he wrote or said in an age so firmly and enthusiastically bound to the love of classical antiquity.

Even as Erasmus began to publish his editions of the pagan clas- sics, he had already turned to the classics of Christianity. In the win- ter of 1500 and through the next year there are scattered references to the work on St. Jerome that was in time to produce his great, authoritative edition of Jerome's letters, to be followed by dozens of editions and commentaries on the other Church Fathers, both Latin and Greek.

Still other writing projects grew from Erasmus's own cultivation of style and from his earlier experience with the instruction of private pupils. The first of such things to be published was his *Adagia*. It was a deceptively simple idea that produced an enormously popular book, one that was to be enlarged and republished many times to become one of the earliest of modern standard reference books. It was to be also the foundation stone of Erasmus's fame as a scholar— a collection of stock phrases, epigrams, maxims, proverbs—in short "adages" culled from the literature of antiquity. He may have started it in some fashion or other before his visit to England. In the spring of 1500, after his return to Paris, he was hard at work on it and the book was printed by Philippi in June. It was undoubtedly a by- product of Erasmus's intensified study at this time, of his rereading of the classic writers and his busy schedule of editorial work, even of the beginning of his Greek studies, although the slim volume of the first edition contained only a handful of references to the new treasures of Greek learning among its 818 entries.

The first edition of the *Adagia* was dedicated to his English friend and patron Lord Mountjoy to whom Erasmus attributed the idea for the compilation. While this was probably no more than a graceful compliment, it does reveal another important aspect of his literary activity, both at this time and throughout his life—the cultivation of patrons. Despite the popularity of his works, and even at the very pinnacle of his fame, Erasmus would never be able to live entirely from the profits of his books. The reading public was simply too limited in the early years of the history of printing; the cost of book production was too high; and neither author nor publisher had the protection of copyright laws. Time after time Erasmus's books would be brought out in unauthorized "pirated" editions that not only paid him nothing but damaged the sale of the legitimate editions. Thus in the early sixteenth century it was still indispensable for authors to solicit patrons. Erasmus was to turn the practice into an art for it was his primary means of sustenance. This, more than anything else, dictated the pattern of his work—the fragmentary publication of his classical editions and translations and the frequent reprinting of previously printed works, with only the slightest changes, often no more than a new prefatory poem or letter of dedication. For each new edition was an opportunity not only for new sales at printers' shops and book fairs, but an opportunity to dedicate the work to some different patron or catch the interest of a new one.

Following the publication of the *Adagia*, the search for patrons as well as a new outbreak of the plague in Paris frequently forced Erasmus to be away from the city and his studies. In 1501–2 he traveled extensively in the Netherlands, trying without much success to regain the good will of the Bishop of Cambrai and using every contact he could muster to find new patrons. His letters to the great and wealthy are polished models of their type—restrained, decorous, flattering, clever or grave, as the occasion dictated—each carefully contrived to strike precisely the right note; those to his friends seeking their help, intercession, or introductions are crisp and candid, alternately desperate and cynical. Especially frustrating was his long negotiation with a wealthy Dutch widow, Anna van Borssele, the "Lady of Veere." Jakob Batt, one of the friends Erasmus had met shortly after entering the service of the bishop, was her chaplain and the tutor to her son. The kind and generous-hearted Batt did his best to gain the lady's support for his friend. Their letters to each other speculate upon what gambits Erasmus should use in approaching her, what flatteries might be especially effective, about her moods and the turn of events in her household. Erasmus considered dedicating the *Adagia* to her son. She was courteous, even friendly: she would seem just on the point of making him some generous gift— and then slip away to give her support to other scholars, preachers, theologians. One of Erasmus' letters expresses his frustration to his friend:

You will point out how much more credit I shall do her by my learning than the other divines whom she maintains. They preach obscure sermons; I write what will live for ever; they, with their ignorant rubbish, are heard in one or two churches; my books will be read in every country in the world; such unlearned divines abound everywhere, men like me are scarcely found in many centuries, unless perhaps you are too scrupulous to tell a few fibs for a friend. You will then point out, that she will be none the poorer, if while so much of her wealth is shamefully thrown away, she devotes a few crowns to the restoration of the works of St. Jerome and the revival of true theology.[29]

Things did not much improve and in the fall of 1502 he wrote despairingly to his old friend Willem Hermans, "This year Fortune has played fine havoc with us"—the Lady of Veere had remarried, the faithful Batt "has been removed by death," as had the wealthy Archbishop of Besançon, François de Busleiden "of whom I had great hopes," and Mountjoy "is cut off from me by the sea."[30] Within a month the Bishop of Cambrai would also be dead.

This letter to Hermans was written from Louvain where Erasmus had gone, probably to cultivate new patrons. He was possibly attracted by the University of Louvain, though he complained of the scarcity of Greek books and its general backwardness. Nevertheless he was shortly pulled into the circle of the university and his fortunes at last began to turn for the better. He was befriended by Adrian Florisze of Utrecht, who would later become Pope Adrian VI and who at this time was already a powerful ecclesiastic, an established theologian, and a high official of the university. Erasmus's reputation for learning apparently had reached Adrian. Through his influence Erasmus was offered an appointment in the university. But he refused Adrian as he had refused Colet—and for the same reason, the urgency of his own studies. He was fortunately able to indulge the luxury of refusal.

Perhaps through Adrian, perhaps on his own initiative, he had come to know Nicholas Ruistre, the Chancellor of the university, Bishop of Arras, and a councillor to Duke Philip of Burgundy. He dedicated his first Greek translation, of Libanius, to Ruistre. He had made friends with the learned and wealthy Jerome de Busleiden, Archdeacon of Cambrai and the brother of the dead Archbishop of Beasançon, whom he had earlier courted. He was the house guest of Jan Desmarez, a fellow poet and humanist and University Orator. These contacts reached outside the university to touch the rich and cultivated Burgundian court. Jakob Mauritsz, a fellow townsman of Erasmus, a learned lawyer, and, like others of the Louvain circle, a councillor to the court, invited him to compose a Latin oration, a Panegyric for Duke Philip upon his return to the Low Countries from a state visit to Spain. Through most of the fall of 1503 he worked intermittently at the task, polishing its periods and fretting over its sentiments and protesting at the time it was taking from more worthwhile work. In January, 1504, Erasmus delivered his oration as part of the splendid occasion of the duke's return, held in the ducal palace in Brussels. He was given the princely sum of a hundred florins. The Panegyric, further polished and expanded, was quickly given to the printer Thierry Martens, to be printed while the occasion was still fresh in peoples' minds. In the course of his stay in Louvain Erasmus had also completed his first major devotional work, the *Enchiridion Militis Christiani*, which we shall examine later, and it had been published by Martens in February, 1503, along with a number of lesser and related pieces under the title *Lucubratiunculae aliquot*. In the spring of 1504, in spite of improving circumstances and his occupation with the translations of Lucian and perhaps as a favor to Adrian or at the urging of his other friends, Erasmus did deliver a series of lectures on rhetoric or poetry at the University of Louvain.

Then in the fall of 1504, in the midst of his burgeoning fortunes, increasing reputation, and growing confidence in his own learning, word reached him that his friend Nicholas Werner, the Prior of Steyn, had died and that Servatius Rogerus had succeeded to his office. This was disquieting news, not only because the old prior had been Erasmus's protector but because Servatius might not be so indulgent with him. The intimate friendship of their early years had cooled. Servatius had apparently forsaken his own literary studies, and he might not understand Erasmus's continued cultivation of literature. Nor might he understand Erasmus's repeated delays and postponements in obtaining the doctoral degree in theology. He might at any moment decide that Erasmus's place was back in Steyn with the brothers he had left more than a decade before. In Louvain Erasmus was too close to Steyn, too vulnerable to the possible discipline of his new prior. By midwinter he was back in Paris, the guest of a well-to-do English cleric, Christopher Fisher. Through Fisher Erasmus was once more in contact with the English circle in Paris and his thoughts turned again to the pleasant recollections of his earlier visit to England, to the friends and scholars there who had affected him so deeply, and to the sense of purpose they had stimulated in him.

His first extant letter, after his return to Paris, is to John Colet and is in the nature of a report on the work and study for the sake of which he had declined Colet's invitation to remain at Oxford and returned to the continent five years before.

I cannot tell you, most excellent Colet, how intensely I long to devote myself to sacred literature, and how disgusted I am with every hindrance and delay. But the unkindness of Fortune, who still regards me with her old disfavour, has prevented me from extricating myself from these entanglements. . . .

He goes on to say that he has returned to Paris in the hopes of better fortune and if matters improve,

I shall then address myself in freedom and with my whole heart to divine studies, in which I mean to spend the remainder of my life. Yet three years ago, I did venture to write something on St. Paul's Epistle to the Romans, and finished with a single effort some four rolls, which I should have continued if I had not been hindered, my principal hindrance being my constant want of Greek.

Thus, the last three years had been "entirely taken up with the study of Greek." And, he reports, he had begun to look at Hebrew "but frightened by the strangeness of the idiom, and in consideration of my age and of the insufficiency of the human mind to master a multitude of subjects, I gave it up."

He has been working on Origen and is much interested in his theology.

He then reports on his writings and notes that he is sending Colet a copy of the *Lucubratiunculas aliquot.*

His hopes to devote himself entirely to sacred studies are, of course, as always bound up with the need to live. He asks Colet to check for him on the matter of "the hundred copies of my Adages which were forwarded to England at my cost not less than three years before."

In some way or other I must contrive to live entirely to myself for several months, in order to get clear of the entanglements I have undertaken in profane literature, a thing I hoped to do this winter, if I had not been disappointed in so many of my expectations. Neither will a great price be required to purchase this freedom, which is a matter of a few months. I beseech you therefore to do what you can to help me in my craving for sacred studies, and to rescue me from that kind of literary work which has ceased to be agreeable to me. I must not ask my lord Mountjoy, although if he came forward to help me of his own good nature, he would not be doing anything out of the way or inappropriate, as he has always encouraged my studies.[31]

This important letter clearly reveals two pressing and closely related preoccupations of Erasmus at this time—his heightened need for financial support and his resolution to turn seriously to sacred scholarship. The latter, of course, depended upon the former and Colet was the key to both. The train of events that had brought Erasmus back to Paris had, for the time being, closed out the prospects for patronage that had begun to materialize in the Low Countries. In Paris his prospects were even more limited. But in England matters might be different. Colet himself was a wealthy man and had just been appointed to the important Deanship of St. Paul's: but equally important, Colet was probably his most influential contact with the English court and church and thus a key figure in any plan to gain substantial English patronage.

At the same time there was no one in the intellectual community— either in England or on the continent—whose approval meant more to Erasmus. Thus his assertions to Colet of the sincerity of his purpose to devote himself to sacred studies were undoubtedly genuine. We must think back to their earlier association, to Erasmus's agreement in principle with Colet's program, and to his own work and study of the intervening five years. In that time he had become a Christian humanist. He had largely perfected his knowledge of Greek. He had, in his work on St. Paul's Epistle to the Romans, made a beginning that would carry through to his New Testament studies that would, within a decade, make him the foremost biblical

scholar of his age. In addition to the study of Origen, he had begun
work on a number of other Church Fathers, the most important being Jerome. He had already started his commentaries on "the whole
works of St. Jerome" within weeks of his return from England in the
winter of 1500,[32] had continued work on him intermittently, and
would complete it during his stay at Cambridge in 1512–13. He may
well have begun, at the same time, the preparation of the definitive
edition of Jerome's letters that would finally appear at the same time
as the Greek New Testament and share its scholarly acclaim. It was
also at about the same time as his long letter to Colet in December,
1504, that Erasmus had completed editing, for the press of Josse
Bade, Lorenzo Valla's *Notes on the New Testament*, the famous
Adnotationes, a manuscript copy of which he had discovered shortly
before returning to Paris and which was to affect so profoundly the
form of his own biblical scholarship.

As the *Adnotationes* issued from the press, Erasmus was making
preparations to go once more to England. Perhaps his appeal to
Colet had borne fruit. We know that some of his other highly placed
English friends had written urging him to come. And there was apparently the promise of an ecclesiastical benefice available to him
there—he hinted broadly to that effect in a hasty letter to his new
prior written several months after his arrival in London in the winter
of 1505.[33] This was an important matter for it would at last give him
a status, position, and income apart from his monastery, and the
freedom and quiet to carry on the work to which he was now committed. On several previous occasions he had expressed a fleeting
hope for such a living—from the Lady of Veere, for example—but
this was the first time the prospect actually seemed a real possibility.

He had, therefore, to come to terms with two serious personal
problems, the claim of his monastery upon him and his illegitimacy.
For, though he had long since been ordained priest, the "defect" of
his birth still prevented him, by the strict terms of canon law, from
holding any church office or living. The solution to both problems—
indeed the only solution—was a papal dispensation. Erasmus set
about to gain it. But how to proceed? Such things were normally
arranged by the sheer exercise of influence, influence exerted through
the complex of personal friendships, debts and favors, and family
connections and nepotism that characterized the papal bureaucracy
and which were generally only available to wealth and high position.
Although Erasmus numbered among his friends and benefactors

several persons of wealth and position, none of them had familiar access to this particular avenue of papal favor. But then he met Andrea Ammonio.

Ammonio was an Italian cleric and humanist adventurer who had come to England in the train of the Italian bishop of the English see of Worcester in 1504. Erasmus probably met him shortly after he arrived in London in the winter of 1505. They struck it off immediately, and, as it turned out, they were able to help each other. Erasmus helped Ammonio secure a position as Latin secretary to Lord Mountjoy. And Ammonio, through the influence of his friends and contacts of his own in Rome, secured Erasmus his much needed dispensation, from Pope Julius II. It was dated January 4, 1506. And the terms were precisely those Erasmus required. He was absolved from the disadvantages of his illegitimate birth; he was allowed "lawfully to hold and keep any ecclesiastical benefice whatsoever"; and relieved from "the statutes and customs of the monastery of Steyn in Holland."[34]

Meanwhile, the benefice for which he had so hopefully returned to England did not materialize; but his English friends were delighted to have him with them once more and generous in their support. Most of them were in London. Thomas More was now married and living in the city and, though he was a rising young lawyer, still eagerly pursued his humanistic studies. He had continued to work at Greek with Grocyn and Linacre. With William Lily, Grocyn's godson and a capable, Italian-trained Greek scholar, More had recently translated into Latin a series of epigrams from the *Greek Anthology*, in friendly literary competition. Erasmus probably spent much of the time of this second visit to England at More's home—mutual friends called them "the twins."[35] The two of them continued the game of translation from Greek, deciding upon Lucian, probably at Erasmus's suggestion since he had already "discovered" that witty ancient satirist. Both men found these exercises diverting. But, most of all, the work probably simply provided another excuse and another device for enjoying each other's company, as Erasmus writes, "to break a lance, as it were in this tourney of wits with the sweetest of all my friends."[36]

With the graceful beggary that had now become almost second nature, Erasmus scattered dedicatory letters to his Lucian pieces. One of them he dedicated to Richard Whitford, a scholar friend but also chaplain to the rich and powerful Richard Foxe, Bishop of

Winchester and advisor to Henry VII. To the bishop himself he dedicated another, and still another to Thomas Ruthall, Dean of Salisbury, another royal councillor. None of these dedications apparently made any immediate return. At about this same time Grocyn introduced Erasmus to William Warham, Archbishop of Canterbury and Chancellor of the realm, who was to become Erasmus's most generous and unfailing patron. But for the moment there was no substantial patronage to be expected from this quarter—nor from any other that he could count on. There was still no living in sight and even the hospitality of his scholar friends wore thin as the months dragged on.

In the spring of 1506 he was induced by Bishop John Fisher, who was Chancellor of Cambridge University and President of Queens' College, to accept the lectureship in theology which the Lady Margaret, the king's mother, had recently endowed. With his usual reluctance at the prospect of teaching, Erasmus accompanied Fisher up to Cambridge in the Easter season of 1506 to receive the king and the queen-mother on a visit there. As Erasmus prepared to take up his distasteful duties at Cambridge he also applied to the university for admission to the Doctor's Degree. The several extensions of his leave from Steyn had all been granted in consideration of his pursuing the doctorate—for almost fifteen years—and we may imagine that the inquiries from Steyn had grown increasingly sharp. While it is true that the dispensation freeing him from the "statutes and customs" of his monastery had already been granted, it is not likely that his superiors there had yet seen it, and we may be assured that Erasmus wanted neither to fight with them nor to have it said that he had not fulfilled his obligations.

But at this point his plans changed again, and he did not pursue the degree at Cambridge. He was invited to accompany the two young sons of Giovanni Battista Boerio, the king's Genoese physician, to Italy. Here at last was the opportunity he had dreamed of! But what of the doctorate? Perhaps this was possible too, for the Boerio boys were bound for Bologna, where Erasmus had earlier expressed the hope of taking his degree. But could he manage it—either the money, the time, or the requirements? He had long since become completely cynical about the substance of the degree but having it was still important. He turned once more to Ammonio and his friends who, in all probability, used their influence with the pope again, this time to dispense Erasmus from the requirements for the doctor's degree.

The arrangements were made, not at Bologna, unfortunately, for the pope was at war with that city, but at Torino, probably before leaving England. The party was ready to depart in the spring of 1506. "The shipman is already in a hurry, and crying out that winds and tides wait on no man," Erasmus wrote excitedly to one of his English friends.[37] At last he was on his way to Italy.

V   *"Causa studiorum perigrinatur": Erasmus's Trip to Italy*

The party—Erasmus, the young Boerios, their English tutor, their servants and retainers—stopped briefly in Paris, probably waiting to join an English royal herald also bound for Italy who, with his escort, was to offer them protection along the way; for travel with a small party was still not entirely safe in the opening years of the sixteenth century. Erasmus employed this several weeks' time in Paris with his old friend the printer Josse Bade. Bade was already at work on a new edition of Erasmus's earlier *Adagia* and Erasmus contributed a few additional items. He also gave Bade the manuscript of his translation of Euripides' *Hecuba*, with an elegant and gracious letter of dedication to Archbishop Warham. He added to the volume another translation of Euripides, the *Iphigenie in Aulis*. For good measure the volume also contained Erasmus's *Prosopopaeia Britanniae*, the poem he had labored over some six years before to present to the boy Prince Henry. He also made arrangements with Bade for the printing of several of his translations of Lucian.

In the late summer Erasmus and his party took up their journey once more, through Orleans, Lyons, and over the pass of Mt. Cenis. The journey, despite the happy anticipation of Italy, was not entirely pleasant. The two Englishmen, the herald and the boys' tutor, quarreled, at one point almost coming to blows with swords drawn, and Erasmus withdrew into his own thoughts. Those thoughts, as if to match the uncongenial company and the "snow buried passes" that surrounded him, turned to "the white hairs in his whiskers," to become part of a poem on old age, written at this time, noting the lines down on a scrap of paper spread across the pommel of his saddle as they came to him, to make "an equestrian, or perhaps I should say an Alpestrian poem."[38] He was, after all, forty years old and far from robust. He could not have anticipated that he would live to be almost seventy or that the fulfillment of his life and work still lay ahead of him.

As they descended into the warm sunshine and early autumn ver-
dance of the north Italian plain Erasmus's mood improved. His com-
panions had composed their quarrel over a bottle of wine and ahead
of them lay Torino, where on September 4, 1506, Erasmus received
the anticipated doctorate in theology by the authority of the Bishop
of Torino and Chancellor of the University, a great-nephew of Pope
Julius. Erasmus wrote immediately to his prior at Steyn, announcing
his degree and even the deprecating tone of his brief, hasty note cannot conceal the importance of the event. At the same time he wrote
Bade in Paris who received the information in time to insert a brief
notice of Erasmus's new dignity at the end of the *Luciani Opuscula* as
it issued from the press.

From Torino Erasmus and his party set out once more at a lei-
surely pace for Bologna. They stopped briefly at Pavia, where Erasmus was not impressed with the magnificence of the Certosa, only
with its extravagance. As they neared Bologna they were forced to
turn aside to Florence for Pope Julius was once more besieging Bologna. Erasmus was apparently as unmoved by the art treasures of
Florence as by those of Pavia. There are only three brief letters extant
from Florence—all written the same day, November 4, all addressed
to friends in the north, probably meant for the same packet of mail:
none of them refers in any way to the artistic wealth, the libraries,
or the great tradition of Renaissance Florence.

Within two weeks Erasmus and his charges, having learned that
Bologna was on the point of surrendering, made their way back,
arriving in time to see the magnificent ceremonial entry of the pope
into the fallen city and Julius himself, as Erasmus wrote, "triumph-
ing, conquering, and playing the part of Julius (Caesar) to perfection."[39] These bitter words record Erasmus's first sight of Pope
Julius II, the man to whom he was so deeply indebted. Erasmus's
disposition to be grateful for the pope's favors was shaken by the
revelation now of what sort of man his benefactor actually was. His
sense of betrayal, perhaps even of complicity, doubtless underscored
the vehemence of his reaction. So profound was the shock of these
impressions that Erasmus would never be quite the same man again.
In this fact lies much of the importance of his experience of Italy,
Margaret Mann Phillips has observed, "it was Julius II who turned
Erasmus into a pacifist."[40] This may well be so. And it may be
equally well argued that it was Julius and the whole jarring shock
of his reaction to the Julian papacy that turned him decisively to the

cause of church reform to which he was to devote the remainder of his life. The visit to Italy thus became one of the major watershed events of his life. From this time onward the antiwar theme became one of the motifs of Erasmus's work and to his last days the terrible image of Julius was fixed in his mind as the standard of Church corruption against which to measure any accomplishment or hope of reform.

The experience of Italy became a watershed event in Erasmus's life in still another way, for it marked the real beginning of his worldwide fame as a scholar. That beginning is tied to Aldus Manutius and the Aldine Press of Venice, the most celebrated publishing house in Europe at the turn of the sixteenth century. Erasmus was well aware, of course, of its celebrity and of the agreeableness and generosity of Aldus through such literary friends as Grocyn and Linacre, both of whom knew him well.

As the months passed in Bologna and Erasmus made friends in its academic community, practiced his Greek, and finally discharged his obligation to the sons of Boerio, he wrote his first letter to Aldus in the fall of 1507. It was exactly the kind of elegant, flattering letter that Erasmus had learned so well how to write. He proposed to Aldus a new edition of the two Greek tragedies he had left with Bade in Paris on the way to Italy. Aldus agreed and the proposed work was quickly printed and ready for the proofreaders, with a new preface—again dedicated to Archbishop Warham.

As the book was being finished Aldus invited Erasmus to come to Venice. After some polite hesitation, he accepted and was shortly welcomed to the press and to Aldus's household, that extended family of craftsmen, printers, proofreaders, editors, and resident scholars which has come to be called the Aldine Academy. Some of its members were already famous men of letters. Janus Lascaris and Marcus Musurus were Greeks, not only eminent scholars but men of the world with far-reaching cultural and political connections. Some, like Jerome Aleander with whom Erasmus shared a room for part of his stay in Venice, were brilliant younger men of scholarly promise. But all of them belonged equally to Aldus's household and to his table where nothing but Greek was spoken, where scholarship and literature were their passions. Here at last was the kind of company Erasmus had imagined to exist in Italy.

In this congenial setting Erasmus proposed to Aldus an expanded version of the *Adagia* on which he had been working again in Bologna. Once more Aldus agreed and the work quickly became a project that caught the imagination of the entire academy. Aldus opened his library to Erasmus as did other Venetian collectors and bibliophiles, friends of the great printer whom Erasmus did not even know. Scholars both within and outside the Aldine circle came forward with Greek manuscripts and texts not yet printed, an incredible, glittering horde of works—Plato, Plutarch, Athenaeus, Homer, Pausanius, Pindar. As Erasmus wrote, recalling the scene many years later, "We began together, I to write and Aldus to print." The shape of the earlier volume, containing only slightly more than eight hundred entries, along with some revision notes—"the confused and indigested material of a future book"[41]—was radically changed. The number of items swelled to more than three thousand, most of them never seen in print before.

The Aldine edition of the *Adagia* was completed in less than nine months. Time had to be taken out for a painful attack of kidney stone that laid Erasmus up for several weeks, the first instance, so he tells us, of the affliction that would plague him for the rest of his life. But the work resumed and at a furious pace. It was done in the midst of the noise and confusion of the press, "We were so busy, that we had hardly time, as they say, to scratch our ears."[42] This was, nevertheless, a scene to be repeated many times. For in the scholarly press Erasmus had found his element, more congenial to him than the study or the classroom.

As the Aldine Euripides had been rededicated to Archbishop Warham, the Aldine *Adagia*—with its proud new title, *Adagiorum Chiliades tres ac centuriae fere totidem*, proclaiming its more than three thousand items—was rededicated to Lord Mountjoy.

From Venice Erasmus went to Padua in the winter of 1508, probably intending to return to the north, but there he met Alexander Stuart, the natural son of James IV of Scotland, an engaging young man of only eighteen, who was already Archbishop of St. Andrews. Erasmus agreed to become his tutor. They combined Alexander's continued studies with the "standard tour" of the antiquities and by slow stages made their way to Rome, where the young archbishop was probably bound to pay a ceremonial visit to the curia. At this point Alexander was called back to Scotland by affairs of state, and Erasmus was left in Rome.

By this time he had contacts of his own there, by way of his patrons and scholar friends from Bologna, Venice, and even England. As in

Bologna and Venice he was welcomed by the circle of the learned in Rome, among them some of the highest officials of the papal court, including the Cardinals Riario and Grimani, and Giovanni Cardinal dei Medici, the future Pope Leo X. Erasmus was as impressed with the grace and learning and generosity of these men and their familiars as he was disenchanted with the secularism, the brutality, and the overt paganism of the court itself—and with Pope Julius.

Then, in the spring of 1509, he received letters from Lord Mountjoy and Archbishop Warham announcing the death of King Henry VII and the accession of his son, the young scholar king Henry VIII. Would Erasmus not return to England to enjoy the patronage, "the mountains of gold" that now seemed so sure a promise? Henry was well disposed to him and had even written him a friendly letter in Bologna. In some respects Erasmus was reluctant to leave Rome. The prospects there were equally attractive, the possibilities both for preferment and scholarship almost unlimited. He later recalled that he did not go to make a last promised call upon Cardinal Grimani lest he be overcome by the cardinal's eloquence and change his mind. But the Christian reformer was already formed in Erasmus, and he probably sensed the need for distance from which to view the center of the Christian world. In any event, he decided to return to England and its promised bounty. He left Italy, never to return.

As he traveled north once more the thoughts of Italy went with him and in the course of the long and tiresome journey they mingled with the thoughts of the good and virtuous English friends he was shortly to see again. The product of this rumination was the *Praise of Folly*. In the letter of dedication to Thomas More he recalled how, as he traveled, the name of More, *Morus*—with whom he expected to stay a while on arriving in London—suggested the sound of the Greek *Moros*, "fool." The Praise of More, "the least foolish of men," perhaps meant as a cheerful little literary guest-gift, thus suggested the *Praise of Folly*, and the most famous of all Erasmus's books was born.

CHAPTER 2

The Court of Folly:
The Satirical Writings of Erasmus

I Moriae Encomium, *the* Praise of Folly

THE *Praise of Folly* was not only Erasmus's most important work of satire: it was also the most popular of all his books. This was true in his own lifetime, despite the formidable reputation of his more weighty writings and his stature as the leading humanist scholar of his age. And it has remained true. The *Moria* went through more than forty editions by some twenty printers before the middle of the sixteenth century, and since that time it has been translated into nearly every language and published in literally thousands of editions.

And yet Erasmus, as we have seen, conceived the book as a diversion on his journey from Rome to London in the summer of 1509 and, as he tells us, actually wrote it in seven days.[1] While this is probably not quite true, it is part of a carefully contrived literary pose, that the work is an improvisation, an impromptu occasional piece. The book takes the form of the classical oration of praise and becomes a verbal satire of its own rhetorical form. Folly uses the form badly—and reminds the reader that she is doing so! She is repetitious and a little disorganized. She neglects prescribed parts of the set oration, including a rousing finish, "I see you are expecting a peroration, but you are certainly foolish if you think that I can remember any part of such a hodgepodge of words as I have poured forth."[2] This sort of thing tends to set the tone of the tumultuous, rattling style that was especially delightful to its contemporary readers, much more responsive than we are today to the stylistic aspect of literary form and steeped in humanist rhetoric.

The *Praise of Folly* is more specifically a further parody of the oration of praise, the praise of such abstractions as Philosophy, Truth, or Wisdom. But in this case it is Folly, making use of a pompous form to celebrate a ridiculous quality. "Yet," she says, "if it is foolish, it is certainly in character; for what is more fitting than that Folly should be the trumpeter of her praises? 'She blows her own horn' " (44). It is the ironic force of this *reductio ad absurdum* that makes the satire work.[3]

In the best style of the classical oration Folly announces her lineage: her father is not Chaos, Saturn, or any of that "senile set of gods," but Plutus, the god of wealth and "the real father of men and gods"; and she was herself begotten on "Youth," "the best looking" and happiest of all the Nymphs (47–48).

With the stage thus set, the goddess proceeds to display her powers. To begin with, she claims power over life itself and the process of conception, for the wisest man "must send for me if he wants to be a father" (49). "I ask, whether the head, the face, the breast, the hand, or the ear—each an honorable part—creates gods and men? I think not, but instead the job is done by that foolish, even ridiculous part which cannot be named without laughter. This is the sacred fountain from which all things rise" (49). Moreover, she continues, what man would stick his head into the noose of marriage or what woman embrace her husband if either really weighed the consequences. She claims all the ages of man from the innocence and joy of childhood to the cheerful, babbling second childhood of senile old age. She claims men and women impartially, and every human relationship. What of the man who thinks his ugly mistress beautiful and "is charmed by the growth on her nose" (57), or the father who believes his cross-eyed son's eyes twinkle (57).

She continues, "There are no great actions without my help, no important arts without my collaboration" (60). She argues that war belongs to her and the arts of government, contending—contrary to Plato—that when philosophers are kings states suffer the most, not only because of the ineptitude of their rulers, but because, by holding resolutely to wisdom, they strip themselves of their common humanity. "I ask you, if it were put to a vote, what city would choose such a person as mayor?" (68). Who would not prefer a fool to whom nothing human is alien?

She claims alchemists, gamblers, artists, noblemen, and all nations and cities. All classes and kinds of men are, in some way, fools and the "Followers of Folly." These include merchants with their "sordid business" and "corrupt methods" (89); grammarians, "a tormented, calamity-ridden God-forsaken body of men" (90), and various other kinds of scholars and poets whose "empty reward is the praise of a handful [and that] obtained only at the cost of ceaseless study and sacrifice" (93); philosophers, and lawyers who "confuse tediousness with brilliance" (94).

This long midsection of the book is the crest of its argument. There had been scattered references to religion and "the religious" throughout the earlier part, but from this point on attention is turned almost exclusively to these subjects. And there is a marked change of tone from bantering good humor to an increasingly savage irony. Folly claims first the theologians with their pride of learning, their reliance upon their "definitions, conclusions, corollaries, and explicit and implicit propositions" (96), their ridiculous quarrels— "It is easier to escape from a maze than from the tangles of Realists, Nominalists, Thomists, Albertists, Occamists, and Scotists, to name the chief ones only" (97)—and with their painfully obvious contrast to the simplicity of the apostles. "The apostles baptized many, although they were never taught the formal, material, efficient and final causes of baptism" (97–98).

Folly next turns to the monks, who "would be very doleful if I did not relieve them in many ways" (101). In addition to their filth, ignorance, and boorishness, she comments upon their punctilious observance of every detail of costume and every requirement of ceremony. "They forget that Christ will condemn all of this and will call for a reckoning of that which He has prescribed, namely, charity" (102). And when the day of judgment comes and the monks present themselves—this one with a "peck of prayers," that one with "enough ceremonies to fill seven ships," and another with "a cowl so dirty and greasy that not even a sailor would wear it" (102–3)— Christ will exclaim, "Whence come this new race of Jews? I acknowledge only one commandment as truly mine, and of that I hear nothing" (103).

From the theologians and monks Folly next turns—after a brief proprietary nod once more in the direction of secular rulers, kings, and nobles—to the rulers of the church, the bishops, cardinals, and popes. And nowhere is she made to speak with such ferocious satiric bite. Her choicest venom, however, is reserved for the popes, the vicars of Christ, so unlike Him in every respect. This section of the book was obviously and profoundly affected by Erasmus's recent trip to Italy and by his observance at first hand of the Julian papacy.

It is from her tirade against the unworthy leaders of the church that Erasmus brings Folly to the conclusion of her address and to the concept of "the Christian Fool." The contrast is a stunning rhetorical coup. Indeed, in the opening passage of this section we see once more the rhetorical parody of the earlier Folly. But this time she is developing the argument that even scripture recognizes the universality, and more, the necessity, of Folly.

What do these things declare except that all men, even the pious, are fools? And that Christ himself, although He possessed the wisdom of the Father, became something like a fool in order to cure the folly of mankind, when he assumed the nature and being of a mortal? And that He was made "to be sin" in order to redeem sinners? He did not wish to redeem them by any way except by the foolishness of the cross, and by weak and simple apostles. These He taught to practice folly and to avoid wisdom. He incited them by the example of children, lilies, mustard-seed, and sparrows, all of them foolish things, living without art or care, by the light of nature alone. (125)

Those who would follow Christ must exemplify the same spirit, for

the Christian religion on the whole seems to have some kinship with folly, while it has none at all with wisdom. If you want proof of this, observe first that children, old people, women, and fools take more delight than anyone else in holy and religious things. . . . Next, you will notice that the founders of religion have prized simplicity exceedingly, and have been the bitterest foes of learning. Finally, no people seem to act more foolishly than those who have been truly possessed with Christian piety. They give away whatever is theirs; they overlook injuries, allow themselves to be cheated, make no distinction between friends and enemies, shun pleasure, and feast on hunger, vigils, tears, labors, and scorn. They disdain life, and utterly prefer death; in short, they seem to have become altogether indifferent to ordinary interests, quite as if their souls lived elsewhere and not in their bodies. What is this, if not to be mad? (127)

And at the end of life, "this is that portion of folly which will not be taken away by the transformation of life, but will be perfected" (131).

It is rather easily observed that, in the course of the *Moria*, Erasmus progressively shifted the meaning of Folly. In the earlier part of the book he is really dealing with simple, relatively harmless self-deception—what today might even be called role-playing.

But Erasmus also includes in his definition of Folly the simplicity of the noble savage in the state of nature—the "golden age" when men "lived without the advantages of learning, being guided by instinct and nature alone . . . free from the insane desire to discover what may lie beyond the stars" (71). And to these he adds those who, so to say, retain the innocence of the state of nature, "those we commonly call morons, fools, nitwits, and naturals" (74), "whose cheerful confusion of mind frees the spirit from care" (76).

Erasmus's own "confusion of mind" and confusion of terms is, of course, no confusion at all but the conscious employment of ambiguity: the very progression of the work depends upon the author's ability to move from one definition to another and ultimately to his concept of "the fool for Christ," for that is the purpose of the book. Both the device and the purpose were readily enough grasped by Erasmus's circle of humanist friends for whom he had originally conceived it. But its purpose was missed, or ignored, by most of the *Moria*'s early critics.

One of them was the conservative theologian Martin van Dorp whom Erasmus had known earlier in Louvain. Dorp wrote to him, complaining that the *Moria* "has excited a great disturbance" and suggesting that he "compose and publish in reply to Folly, a Defence of Wisdom."[4] Dorp failed entirely to see that this is precisely what the *Praise of Folly* was, in the sense that Christian wisdom is the folly of the cross. But Erasmus took considerable pains to respond to Dorp in a lengthy letter not only to explain how he meant the work to be understood but the extent to which it was consistent with his other, more obviously serious writings:

The ideas in *The Praise of Folly* are exactly the same as those in my other essays, but here they are presented ironically (*via diversa*). . . . under the pretext of a eulogy, I approached obliquely the same ideas that I elsewhere have presented directly.[5]

Dorp was never truly convinced nor were most of *Folly*'s other critics, despite the best efforts of Erasmus, his friends, and defenders. Not only was this true of the *Praise of Folly* but of many of Erasmus's other writings. For the ambiguity that baffled Dorp and was so strongly marked a characteristic of the *Praise of Folly* tended more and more to become a central feature of Erasmus's mind and style. It has also been called a taste for paradox, a tendency to present arguments "on the one hand" and "on the other."

The Erasmian taste for paradox owes much to the influence of the satirist Lucian. Erasmus's increasing preference for the pseudo-dramatic form of the dialogue as a vehicle of expression is probably, at least in part, owing to the influence of Lucian. His choice of the declamation—a dramatic monologue—as the form in which to write the *Praise of Folly* is a case in point: his use of the "theater of the world" figure is specifically taken from Lucian's *Icaromenippus* (p. 90, n. 59). But the ironic spirit of Lucian was even more congenial to Erasmus than the examples of his rhetorical usage, and it was more deeply influential. Erasmus has been aptly called the supreme Lucianist of the Renaissance.

The influence of Lucian in the *Praise of Folly* is only a part of the allusive richness of the book. This derives, of course, from Erasmus's general mastery of the classics, but it owes a good deal also to the fact that he had just completed the greatly expanded Aldine edition of the *Adagia*—he makes specific reference to it in the *Moria* (115). Thus there is scarcely a line of the *Praise of Folly* that does not contain a reference or two to the Greek or Latin authors. Indeed, the very excess of classical allusion, Folly's tumbling out and heaping up of examples, is part of the verbal-formal parody to which we referred earlier. This is true also of the argumentation in which Folly pushes the absurdity of the rhetorical tradition of persuasion to its full limit, as when she proves that she has jurisdiction even over prudence, arguing from the figure of the classical Sileni that appearance and reality are really reversed (64–65), or when she argues "that the happiest creatures are those which are least artificial and most natural," that Gryllus (the companion of Ulysses who was changed by Circe into a pig) was considerably wiser than Ulysses and that the fool is to be preferred to be the wise man (72 ff).

Erasmus was, however, not only a classical but a Christian scholar. And, as we have seen, the ultimate purpose of the *Praise of Folly* was the reform of Christian behavior and Christian institutions. That purpose could not be served without coming to grips with the Christian tradition. At the opening of the long final section on "The Christian Fool," Folly calls upon the testimony of Holy Scripture, as earlier she had called upon the authority of the classics. She calls also upon the tutelary spirit of Scotus "more thorny than a porcupine or hedgehog" (117) and treats his followers, the traditional scholastic theologians, with withering contempt. But she makes an exception of "some of the more human divines" who "condemn as a kind of sacrilege . . . this tendency to speak with unclean lips about sacred things [and] to defile the majesty of divine theology with pedantic and wordy language" (99). This was, of course, the theological reform party to which Erasmus himself belonged, along with his English friend John Colet and a handful of other theologians and biblical scholars. The last section of the *Praise of Folly* thus becomes a demonstration of the new, reformed theology and a forecast of the new Christian Humanism of which Erasmus would shortly be the greatest luminary.[6]

II *The* Julius Exclusus

The second most important single satiric work of Erasmus was the dialogue called *Julius exclusus*, closely related to the *Praise of Folly* and written some two years after the *Folly* was published. The occasion that prompted the work was almost certainly the news of the death of Pope Julius II in February of 1513.

Erasmus was at Cambridge, where he had finally gone to take up again the lectureship Bishop Fisher had offered him before he left for Italy, when the glowing hopes for patronage that had brought him back to England had failed completely to materialize. He was bored and fretful in the remote English university town, surrounded by "Thomists and Scotists," and separated from his English humanist friends most of whom were now in London. His thoughts still often turned, as his letters indicate, to the things he had seen in Italy, and in particular to the scandal of the Julian papacy. Thus, when he heard that Julius was dead, what was more natural than to think of him, pounding at the gate of heaven, demanding admittance? The thought produced the dialogue—its principal characters Julius and his Genius (outside the gate) and St. Peter (inside), its substance the argument over whether Julius was to be admitted or excluded, the *exclusus* of the title.

The *Julius* is a curious little book with an even more curious history. It was never published by Erasmus and not only never claimed by him but vigorously denied. Nevertheless, it was his. Several friends, including Thomas More, were aware of the existence of manuscript copies and one of these—we are not sure which—found its way to the printers and was published.[7] Anonymous printed editions began to appear about 1517, part of the glut of pamphlet literature that was one of the staples of early sixteenth century printing.

It proved to be extremely popular and was repeatedly reprinted by any number of publishers. The book caused a terrible furor, led by the same conservative theologians who disliked the *Praise of Folly* and distrusted the liberal theological views that Erasmus had already begun to express not only in his satiric writings but, as we shall see, also in his editorial works and biblical and patristic commentaries. Many of these critics were convinced that Erasmus had written the *Julius*, for, even though they were not aware of the external evidence for his authorship, the similarities of style and point of view between this work and others of Erasmus's, the *Praise of Folly* in particular, were simply too striking to be accidental. But Erasmus persisted in his denials, and his critics were never able to prove conclusively that he wrote it.

There are good reasons to believe that Erasmus never intended the book as anything more than a private document for a narrow circle of friends to see and that its publication was a genuine and serious embarrassment to him. It opened him to charges of the basest ingratitude, for he had received important favors from Pope Julius, as we have seen. He also needed the help of Julius's successor Leo X not only in the matter of a further dispensation but as patron and protector of Erasmus's Greek New Testament, which had just been published.

But there were serious reasons inherent in the *Julius* itself that made Erasmus reluctant to claim it. In one of his several letters denying its authorship, he wrote:

It is true that I "played the fool" in the *Folly*—but bloodlessly! I have never injured the reputation of anyone by name. I have satirized the *mores* of men, not their reputations.[8]

This he could no longer claim if he acknowledged the *Julius*. He saw clearly the difference between the *Moria* and the *Julius exclusus*. Folly had certainly attacked papal abuse, papal secularism, the popes' preoccupation with war. The figure of Julius II was recognizable enough when Folly spoke of "our popes [neglecting] everything else to devote themselves to war" or of "tired old men [acting] with youthful energy and [disregarding] all labor and expense, simply in order to overturn laws, religion, peace, and humane institutions" (113). But the *Julius* was an extended personal attack upon the name, memory, and reputation of the pope himself. In the course of it Julius was accused of illegitimacy, drunkenness, lechery, and un-

natural vice—and, incidentally, of suffering from syphilis—of si-
mony, bribery, and assorted similar forms of personal corruption.

In more general terms, while both the *Praise of Folly* and the
Julius exclusus attacked many of the same papal abuses, Folly had
done it with graceful, if sometimes savage, irony. And, though the
Julius has much of this same ironic spirit—indeed the whole work
is a play upon the one simple and outrageous irony, that the pope
cannot get into heaven!—still the result is not the irony of the *Praise
of Folly*. It is rather the most malicious kind of invective satire. It
is completely lacking in the ambiguity that Folly had so skillfully
employed. This is due in part to the fact that the book, as we have
seen, was never intended for publication, certainly not in the form in
which it was published. In his reference to having seen a manuscript
copy of it, Thomas More, for example, calls it a draft—his phrase is
tantum scriptio, "only a scribble."⁹ Like the first version of the *Praise
of Folly* it was a quickly written, fast-running piece for the amusement
of Erasmus's English friends. But unlike the *Praise of Folly*, it was
never completed, polished, or really prepared for the press. It thus
remained rough and mean, filled with the "cruel and dirty words"
that were part of the invective tradition,¹⁰ and much more direct
about the abuses of papal power, much more explicit about church
reform and ecclesiastical government than it was Erasmus's custom
to be. On the other hand, it is of more than casual interest to have
such a work in such a state of preparation. Even in draft form,
truncated and unedited as it is, it is still a powerful piece of writing,
surely made more so because Erasmus had no time to be evasive.

The central theme of the work is the contrast between Pope Julius
and St. Peter, obviously suggesting the strong contrast between the
historic apostolic church and the contemporary state of ecclesiastical affairs. It must be remembered that Erasmus was already at
work on his monumental edition of the Greek New Testament and
the letters of St. Jerome and that all his writings of these years,
whether clearly serious or apparently trivial, are the documents of
that inner purpose Erasmus called his Philosophy of Christ. The
Julius no less than the *Praise of Folly* must be interpreted in terms
of this emerging philosophy which endowed both these powerful
satiric works with their purpose.

As in the *Praise of Folly*, literary form is made to serve satiric
purpose in the *Julius*. Even more than the *Moria* it seems an improvisation, for the form of the dramatic dialogue permits the argument to flow back and forth in the apparently haphazard manner

of conversation, with interruptions, repetitions, digressions. But it is only apparent: in reality Erasmus is employing a device to stress the point of the dialogue by repetition.

The opening lines set the scene as Julius stands before heaven's gate, fuming; and the baffled St. Peter wonders who is making such a disturbance.

It must be some giant or satrap, a sacker of cities, has arrived. But, immortal God, what a sewer I smell here. I won't open the door right away, but I'll look out of the barred window here and find out what this portent may be. "Who are you? And what do you want?"[11]

Julius is amazed that Peter does not recognize the triple crown and the papal robe "shining all over with jewels and gold," and most of all himself, "the famous Julius the Ligurian . . . Pontifex Maximus" (46–47). But Peter sees nothing he recognizes as any form of holiness either in Julius or in the motley army crowded behind him of "mercenary brigands, or even specters from Tartarus . . . swarmed here from the underworld, to make war on heaven" (48).

Peter remains adamant against Julius's threats, and they settle down to the substance of the dialogue. Peter demands "a recital of your merits," and Julius's first long speech follows. His account of his merits is, of course, a condemnation of his secularism, how "I fought my way to this position" by bribery and corruption, how "in my pontificate . . . there is no one . . . to whom the Church, to whom Christ himself, owes so much as to me" (51–52). He continues to describe his manipulation of papal finance and, "to get to bigger things," his struggle to restore the Papal States and drive the French out of Italy.

Peter is amazed at what has happened to the papacy since his time and his questioning prompts Julius to a long speech in which he is made to present the most extravagant claims for the power of the pope no matter how unworthy or even criminal he may be.

Against the protest of Peter that this is behavior more fitting to Satan than to the Vicar of Christ, Julius angrily responds, "What is more apostolic than to enlarge the Church of Christ?" And to Peter's assertion that what is meant is the enlargement of its spiritual dominion, Julius replies:

Perhaps you are still dreaming of that old Church, in which you and a few starveling bishops ran a really frigid Pontificate, subject to poverty, sweat, dangers, and a thousand nuisances. Time has changed everything for the better. The Roman Pope is now quite a different thing; you were Pope in name and title only. What if you could see today . . . the supreme Pontiff being carried high in the air in a golden chair by soldiers, and everyone worshiping him all along the way as he waves his hand; if you could hear the booming of cannon, the noise of horns, the blare of trumpets, if you could see the flash of artillery, hear the applause of the people, their shouting, see everything glowing in torchlight, and even the most powerful princes having difficulty being admitted to kiss the blessed feet. . . . if you had witnessed even one of my triumphs . . . you would have said that the Scipios, the Aemilii, the Augusti were miserable cheapskates compared to me. (83–84)

The foregoing passage sets the stage for the long, cumulative speech of St. Peter that concludes the book and spells out the contrast between the shape of the papacy in the hands of Julius and the form Christ and the apostles intended for it. Julius is scored for his warmongering, for his glory-seeking at the expense of the true glory of the church: Peter recalls that the deeds of which Paul boasts are "shipwrecks, chains, lashes, perils" (85) and not the triumphs of arms; that Christ himself enjoined man "to spurn all pleasures like poison, to trample on wealth as if it were dirt, to consider life as nothing" (86), that he wanted his church "unencumbered and unburdened by any worldly possessions." "Now, by contrast, I see the man who wants to be regarded as next to Christ and, in fact, equal to Him, submerged in the filthiest of all things by far: money, power, armies, wars, alliances—not to say anything at this point about his vices." "You bless others, yourself accursed; to others you open heaven, from which you yourself are locked out" (87–88).

And so Julius departs from the door of heaven a little chastened but not much, and vowing to return and mount a full-scale assault when "I have built up my forces," when "scores of thousands of men will be butchered in battle and join with me" (90).

III *The* Colloquies

In spite of the furor raised by the *Julius exclusus* and the great popularity of the *Praise of Folly*, by far the most often reprinted of Erasmus's books and the one with the greatest variety of editions was the *Colloquies*. It was also the most effective in spreading his ideas.

Unlike the *Praise of Folly* and the *Julius*, both of which were meant from the beginning as satires, the *Colloquies* were not. They began, as the title implies, as a series of simple exercises in Latin conversation, composed during the late 1490s when Erasmus was at the University of Paris, for the use of the tutorial pupils he took to supplement his income. A friend and fellow student from those Paris days, Augustin Vincent Caminade, had kept a copy which came into the hands of Erasmus's friend and publisher, the Basel printer Johann Froben, to be published as the first edition of the *Colloquies* in November, 1518, under Erasmus's name but without either his knowledge or consent. Indeed Erasmus claimed he no longer even had a copy of the book himself and was rather annoyed with Froben. For the book was badly printed and full of embarrassing errors. Nevertheless, it was immediately popular, even in Froben's defective edition, and was reprinted several times by Froben himself and picked up by other publishers within the next few months. Then, early in 1519, Erasmus prepared a corrected edition for the printer Thierry Martens of Louvain.

The popularity of the *Colloquies* is not hard to explain, even in the modest form of its earliest edition: it was an effective little manual of conversational style, the necessary beginning steps toward the Latin fluency that characterized anyone with the slightest pretention to education in the early sixteenth century. Most of the book was thus given over to simple sentences and conventional phrases— greetings to one's friends and family, "Greetings with good measure, my uncle,"[12] greetings of endearment, greetings of courtesy appropriate to various occupations and social estates, "Hail to your Holiness, Honor, Highness, Beatitude, Sublimity" (559), forms of farewell, forms of inquiry on first meeting or to one in poor health, forms of typical domestic conversation, expressions of thanks, how to invite a friend to lunch. Despite the necessarily formulaic nature of such matter, this little book was clearly and refreshingly different from the many other similar manuals. It owed nothing to them: it grew instead entirely out of Erasmus's own experience, out of his feeling for dialogue and his own mastery of Latin style, out of his genius for easy, lively, flowing conversation. Indeed, even the earliest colloquies may well recall bits of actual conversation, with their flashes of Erasmian wit and anecdote. There is, among the forms of inquiry on first meeting, an exchange referring to Erasmus's unhappy experience at the Collège de Montaigu, which he was to develop more fully in a later colloquy.

George. Just what coop or cave do you come to us from?
Livinus. Montaigu College.
George. Then you come to us full of learning.
Livinus. Oh, no—full of lice. (563)

Even in the earliest editions there was an occasional instance of the satiric bite and reforming purpose that would come to characterize the later colloquies. In the conversation on the forms of inquiry to one in poor health, one of the speakers notes that some have recovered from an illness by putting on a Dominican or Franciscan cowl, to which another responds, "Perhaps the same thing would have happened had they put on a pimp's cloak" (566).

This sort of thing—the timely, irreverent, or ironic comment on contemporary issues—enhanced the popularity of the *Colloquies* and caused the publication of more and more unauthorized editions, taking advantage of the demand with no advantage accruing to the author. For this reason, in part, Erasmus shortly adopted the practice of issuing new editions of the *Colloquies*, as he had done earlier, and continued to do, with editions of his popular *Adagia*.

Beginning with the Froben edition of March, 1522, Erasmus added ten new colloquies. As soon as unauthorized versions of this edition began to appear, he issued another, later in the same year, with yet another entirely new colloquy. This practice continued on an almost yearly basis for the next decade, producing by the last complete edition of 1533, some sixteen editions along the way and by his death, three years later, nearly a hundred editions in all, authorized and unauthorized, partial or complete. In the process the *Colloquies* themselves had grown from the original juvenile manual of some eighty pages to a large, heavy book, almost sixty colloquies having been added over the years, which formed the real substance of the work. It was, in his own lifetime, and continued to be, one of the most widely read books ever written. It was used as a school text in dozens of humanist schools all over Europe, from Cracow to Lisbon. In addition, it was almost equally widely read out of the schoolroom and became one of those books that educated people were simply expected to know. Dozens of major literary figures borrowed from it, Rabelais, Webster, Jonson, perhaps even Shakespeare. The famous soliloquy of Rostand's Cyrano on his nose is an almost literal borrowing from the colloquy "In Pursuit of Benefices."

It is clear that Erasmus's constant additions to the *Colloquies* were more than an attempt to protect the author's market. From the Froben edition of 1522 Erasmus had begun to take the book seriously, to add new and important material, and to go beyond the sketchy conversations of the original version to fully developed little microdramas in which he expressed his views on dozens of things— customs and fashions, the foibles of society, love and marriage and celibacy, literary tastes and practices, the church, and moral and religious questions. These substantial later colloquies owe as little to literary or formal antecedents as did the original version of the work. With only two or three fragmentary exceptions they are taken from the sights and sounds of the time, for which Erasmus had such a sharp eye and retentive ear and which he could depict so convincingly. There are bits of obviously real conversations. There are scenes thoroughly familiar to many of his readers—the steaming stench of the commonroom of a German inn and the meticulous description of the famous English shrines of the Virgin at Walsingham and of St. Thomas Becket at Canterbury. There are encounters with a prostitute, a lamed mercenary, a bogus nobleman, a cheating horse trader, a frightened little boy who can't get his pen sharpened or manage his ink well in a classroom where dictation has already started. There are a dozen scenes of dinner parties, one of them featuring Erasmus's sharp-tongued old housekeeper, Margaret. People bought the successive editions of the *Colloquies* certainly, in part, as much for the freshness and originality of the way in which Erasmus presented his ideas as for what he meant to convey by them. There is surely no other book in the western literary tradition quite like the *Colloquies*.

Some of the individual colloquies that were added, from the 1522 edition on, continued to relate to rhetorical instruction and education, such as "Sport" or "The Whole Duty of Youth," prepared for the 1522 edition, or "The Art of Learning," written in 1529 for Erasmus's godson and namesake, Erasmius Froben.

A number of the colloquies deal, directly or indirectly, with the education of women, a subject on which Erasmus had both strong and liberal views. The most substantial of these is "The Abbot and the Learned Lady" (1524). It is made to carry double freight (as are many others), for its point is enhanced by Erasmus's heavily ironic portrait of the abbot, who may well have been one of his hostile critics, the English Bishop of St. Asaph, Henry Standish, whom in another place he called "the Bishop of St. Jackass." The learned lady is, in all probability, Margaret Roper, Thomas More's daughter. As the lady of the dialogue (Magdalia) welcomes the abbot (Antronius) to her home, he is scandalized to see that "the whole place is filled with books"—"Greek and Latin ones" at that! (219)—and he observes that "It's not feminine to be brainy. A lady's business is to have a good time" (219). Magdalia replies, "Shouldn't everyone live well? Who can have a good time without living well?" Antronius answers, "Rather, who can enjoy himself if he *does* live well? (219). He goes on, "I wouldn't want my monks to spend their time on books," for if they do, they become "less tractable; they talk back by quoting from decrees and decretals, from Peter and Paul" (220).

They return to the question of learning for women, the abbot still unmoved, "Books ruin women's wits—which are none too plentiful anyway" (222). But, says Magdalia, the plain facts show that many more ruin their wits by "intemperate wining and dining, night-long bouts of drunkenness, uncontrolled passions" (222). And, she goes on, the number of learned women is increasing everywhere, "we'll preside in the theological schools, preach in the churches, and wear your miters" (223). "God forbid!" says the abbot, and in closing, invites his hostess to visit him and he'll show her a proper time, "We'll dance, drink as much as we please, hunt, play games, and laugh!" (223). Her parting shot is, "I feel like laughing even now" (223).

In addition to those colloquies dealing with the education of women and with learned ladies there are a number dealing with other women's concerns. One of the most passionate is "A Marriage in Name Only, or The Unequal Match" (1529), the account of an arranged marriage between an innocent young girl and an old rake suffering from syphilis. In "The Girl with No Interest in Marriage" (1523) and "The Repentant Girl" (1523) he argues for a more equal role for women in deciding upon marriage, and in "Courtship" (1523) he creates a delightfully vivacious and strong-minded young woman who will not be rushed into an irrevocable choice.

These liberal feminist opinions were viewed with a special suspicion and hostility by many of the same religious conservatives who opposed Erasmus's liberal views on a broad range of topics. They saw his feminist views, quite correctly, as part of a larger argument Erasmus had developed from his first important devotional work, the *Enchiridion* (1501), through the *Colloquies*, and culminating in the *Institutio Christiani Matrimonii* (1526) and the *Vidua Christiana* (1529) that virtuous Christian marriage is not only parallel to clerical celibacy but is to be preferred to it. They saw, again correctly, that such opinions were corollary to his well-known hatred of monasticism.

Part of the hostility grew from the suspicious similarity between such Erasmian secularism and the growing Lutheran tumult of the 1520s. Luther had, after all, written his tract against the sacraments, *On the Babylonian Captivity of the Church*, in 1520. Clergy in Wittenberg and other places in Germany were already beginning to abandon their vows and take wives by 1521–22, and in 1525 Luther himself married. On these matters, as others, it made no difference to Erasmus's critics that he had expressed himself decisively twenty years before Luther was heard of.

All of this leads us into the largest and most important group of the colloquies, those devoted to religion, the church, and related objects of Erasmus's anger and ridicule. They were written mainly in the decade of the 1520s when Erasmus was in the midst of controversy with Luther, Zwingli, and other reformers on the one hand and a host of conservative Catholic apologists on the other. In spite of the increasing polarity of religious issues, in spite even of the fact that Erasmus himself was finally obliged to speak out publicly against Luther in 1524–25, as we shall see, he steadfastly maintained in the colloquies of the 1520s his advocacy of a middle position between the hostile factions. Even as he was at work on his tract against Luther, *On Free Will*, he wrote the colloquy "An Examination Concerning Faith" for the Froben edition of March, 1524. It is a straightforward, orthodox exposition of the Apostles' Creed. But he makes one of its speakers clearly represent himself and the other either Luther or a Lutheran spokesman. And the thrust of the dialogue is that in spite of hostility on some issues, there are many important things still held in common between Luther and the Catholic community, not least the Apostles' Creed itself, and that such areas of agreement can still be made the basis for peaceful compromise.

In most of this group of colloquies he takes the position that the abuses, errors, excesses, and derelictions of the church are no less real and no less the continuing concern of orthodox Catholics for having been attacked by heretics.

As early as the March, 1522, Froben edition, in the colloquy "In

Pursuit of Benefices," he deplored the same scandalous pluralism that Luther had attacked in his *Address to the Christian Nobility of the German Nation*. In "Rash Vows," prepared for the same edition, Erasmus dealt with the worthlessness of indulgences, although the condemnation of Luther, arising in part out of his attack upon indulgences, had just occurred at the Imperial Diet of Worms. But Erasmus's questioning of indulgences in "Rash Vows" grew out of his more direct attack in that colloquy upon the worthlessness of pilgrimages and the indulgence value attached to them.

His most famous attack on pilgrimages, however, was his colloquy "A Pilgrimage for Religion's Sake" (1526). It is based loosely upon personal experience, Erasmus's visit some years earlier to the Shrine of the Virgin at Walsingham and to that of St. Thomas Becket at Canterbury in the company of his austere English friend John Colet. But these two shrines are only examples of the general practice of the cult of saints and relics which had become so widespread and so abused as to be condemned by many serious-minded Catholics as well as by Luther and Lutheran sympathizers. Indeed, one of the speakers of the colloquy refers to "this new-fangled notion that pervades the whole world" (288) and notes that it has cut seriously into the gifts given to the saints and may threaten the whole cult of saints. But it is not the purpose of Erasmus's satiric attack to second the views of Luther nor to attack basic doctrine. It is rather to reform corrupt practice and strengthen true Christian doctrine. Thus, the display of a vial of the Virgin's milk at Walsingham leads one of the speakers to doubt that she could have produced so much, displayed here and there at one shrine after another. His companion notes that there is so much wood of the true cross "which is exhibited publicly and privately in so many places that if the fragments were joined together they'd seem a full load for a freighter" (295).

"Exorcism, or The Specter" (1524) was directed at the ignorance and superstition of many clergy as well as, to some extent, at the concept of exorcism itself which Erasmus considered a questionable doctrine.

In "A Fish Diet" (1526), the obvious target of the satire is the conventional Christian prohibition against eating meat on holy days. To that end the chief speakers are a butcher and a fishmonger, themselves small masterpieces of comic invention. Again, as in the other colloquies of the same period, this one can be related to the din of controversy raised by the Lutherans, Zwingli, and other reformers over fasting and dietary laws in the early 1520s. But, as in so many other cases, Erasmus's concern with this question both predates the contemporary controversy, and goes beyond it to the larger matter, really, of Christian liberty. The colloquy is filled with satiric jibes at the ridiculous observance of trifles in religion. The butcher, for example, repeats a story about a pregnant nun who claims she was raped. But when asked why she didn't cry out, she answers, "I would have done so, but there's a strict rule against making noise in the dormitory" (344). Erasmus makes the fishmonger speak for him recalling the savage asceticism he had endured in his own school days at the Collège de Montaigu in Paris, ending with the observation, "Who would deny that this was cruelty to a fellow human?" (352).

"The Shipwreck" (1523) is one of the most enduringly popular of all the colloquies. Craig R. Thompson considers it among "the best satirical writing produced in the sixteenth century" (139). Like most of Erasmus's satires its effectiveness is heightened by its literary quality and the tumultuous, breakneck pace of the narrative, vividly conveying the confusion of action and the terror of the events that form the nexus of the dialogue. Even the minor characters who are barely sketched in the narrative have life and character and substance. Adolph, the narrator, is telling his friend Antony of his narrow escape from a storm at sea and a shipwreck. While the precise choice of the setting may reflect a shipwreck that Erasmus actually heard of, it may also be either a literary borrowing or totally imaginary. It was chosen principally as a convincing crisis situation in which to depict faith under stress. The depiction reaches its point, as does the satire, when, as the fury of the storm mounts, the captain announces that the ship is about to sink and "warns each of us to commend himself to God and prepare for death" (140).

Sailors and passengers alike pray to the Virgin Mary under all the names that tradition attaches to her. Some make vows to one or another of her shrines. Some even try to placate the sea directly—an Erasmian jab at the crude pantheism often concealed under the guise of the saints—"O most merciful sea, O most kind sea, O most splendid sea, O most lovely sea, have pity on us! Save us!" (141).

Some pledged themselves to become Carthusians. There was one who promised to journey to St. James at Compostella barefoot, bareheaded, clad only in a coat of mail, begging his bread besides. (141)

Adolph continues,

> I couldn't help laughing as I listened to one chap, who in a loud voice (for fear he wouldn't be heard) promised a wax taper as big as himself for the Christopher in the tallest church in Paris—a mountain rather than a statue. While he was proclaiming this at the top of his lungs, insisting on it again and again, an acquaintance who chanced to be standing by nudged him with his elbow and cautioned: "Be careful what you promise. Even if you sold all your goods at auction, you couldn't pay for it." Then the other, lowering his voice—so Christopher wouldn't hear him, of course!—said, "Shut up, you fool. Do you suppose I'm serious? If I once touch land, I won't give him a tallow candle." (142)

In contrast, Adolph himself, refusing to "make deals with saints" (142), was quietly praying to God. And as other passengers clamored to make confession to an old priest and a Dominican aboard, Adolph "confessed silently to God, condemning my unrighteousness before him and imploring his mercy."

> Antony.   Where would you have gone had you died in that condition?
> Adolph.   That I left to God the Judge, for I was unwilling to be judge of my own cause; nevertheless a strong hope possessed my mind the whole time. (143)

In the meantime, the priest and the Dominican had crowded into the already overcrowded lifeboat which was swamped and sank. In contrast, Adolph describes the calmness of a young mother with her baby who was tied to a broken plank and made it safely to shore. And, of course, Adolph, too, was saved, clinging to the stump of the mast along with the old priest.

Conservative Catholic theologians—many of them already critical of Erasmus's Greek New Testament and his biblical commentaries and suspicious of the views expressed in many of his religious and devotional writings and of what they considered the mocking, "paganizing" tone of such books as the *Praise of Folly*—were even more offended by the *Colloquies*. As early as 1522 the Inquisitor of Louvain objected to the book on the ground of its "Lutheran" tendencies. In 1526, Erasmus's enemies at the Sorbonne gained an official censure by that influential faculty against sixty-nine passages in the *Colloquies* and in others of his writings as "erroneous, scandalous, or impious," and it was forbidden to be used for instruction "lest under the pretext of instructing [students] it corrupt their morals."[13]

This was a serious matter and for the next edition of the *Colloquies*—within a month after the condemnation—Erasmus wrote a full-dress defence, "The Usefulness of The *Colloquies*." He argued that the book was not a piece of systematic theology and should not be treated "as if the dogmas of the Christian creed were solemnly spelled out in [its] pages!" (625). He argued further that he had done no more than to add to a harmless little book on the refinements of language," here and there, "some passages to direct the mind toward religion," and that far from being a pernicious book, the *Colloquies* was useful to Christian piety, that it promoted rather than undermined true religion.

In "Rash Vows" and "A Pilgrimage for Religion's Sake" he claimed only to have pointed out the abuses connected with the excessive zeal for pilgrimage which takes people from their proper vocations and uses religion "as a cover for superstition, faithlessness, foolishness, and recklessness" (626). He reminds his critics that St. Jerome had said that to have visited Jerusalem was not as important as to have lived righteously. He defended both the doctrine and the method of the several colloquies dealing with marriage, pointing out that there are many ways in which men have tried to teach the precepts of Christianity and that there are always "those sour natures who are lacking in every grace, and to whom anything friendly and gay seems immodest" (628). As to "Exorcism," he was simply trying by "an amusing example" (630) to expose ignorance and charlatanism. He argued further that he had not universally condemned the religious orders, pointing to his sympathetic portrayal of the monk in "The Soldier and the Carthusian" and that, moreover, if the orders are so sensitive to their honor, let them correct the practices of their worst members rather than slandering one who holds those practices up to ridicule.

In the same vein he claims that he has not everywhere disapproved of fasting or of the intercession of the Virgin and the saints any more than he universally condemned the orders. He adds, moreover, that, for example, in "A Pilgrimage for Religion's Sake," "I reproach those who with much ado have thrown all images out of the churches" (631). He defends himself by claiming that the offensive opinions sometimes expressed in the *Colloquies* cannot be uniformly attributed to him, that they rather belong to the characters speaking them, and that they serve dramatic effect as a foil for other opinions of other characters. If, as in "Youthful Piety," a soldier or a drunkard is made to condemn fasting, "does that make Erasmus a condemner of fasts? I think not!" (634).

Despite the ingenuity of his arguments, despite even the irenic note on which he ended his defence, an appeal to "the peacemaker among all men, the Holy Spirit, who employs his instruments in divers ways, [to] make us all united and of one accord in sound doctrine and godly living" (637), Catholic conservative opinion continued to object to the *Colloquies*. The Sorbonne condemned it again in 1528, and in the following year the faculties of canon law and medicine of the University of Paris joined in the condemnation. There were condemnations and censures against the book in Louvain, Cologne, and various places in Spain. Individual church officials objected to all or part of it; even Erasmus's old friend Cuthbert Tunstall, now Bishop of London, joined in the censure of "A Fish Diet" in 1529. Reasons for this continuing opposition are not hard to find. For, despite Erasmus's disingenuous claims to the contrary, the main thrust of the *Colloquies* was indeed against monasticism, the mendicant orders, the ignorance and superstition of the clergy, the emptiness and worthlessness of the external practices of religion without their informing spirit. In more instances than not, his criticisms agreed with those of the increasingly vocal Protestant reformers at the very time orthodox Catholic apologists were calling for a closing of ranks. Erasmus's argument that he was not necessarily responsible for the opinions of speakers in his dialogues—the same argument he had used against the critics of the *Praise of Folly*— only succeeded in further irritating his critics, especially as they often fancied they saw themselves held up to ridicule in the *Colloquies*, under one transparent guise or another. And, of course, they were even more enraged when their condemnations only succeeded in increasing the book's popularity, promoting its sales, and producing edition after edition.

IV   The Ciceronian

This was the last of Erasmus's major satirical works. It was closely related to the *Colloquies*: indeed it was first widely circulated in the 1529 edition of the *Colloquies*, but thereafter was separately published. It was also closely related to the bitter controversies of the late 1520s over the *Colloquies*, over Erasmus's social and religious views as expressed in various of the colloquies and elsewhere, and over Erasmus's relation to, and responsibility for, the Lutheran tumult. Not only had these questions been raised in northern Europe but in Italy, even in the Roman *curia*. This was a particularly dangerous situation. Erasmus had been put under considerable pressure to come out strongly against Luther. In response to that pressure and to his own growing disquiet over the radical drift of Lutheranism he had written his *On Free Will* (1525). But most of his critics were not satisfied, nor were the chief spokesmen of the papacy, for Erasmus continued to deploy his criticism of clerical abuses, of questionable church doctrines, and of the excesses of popular religious practice, in spite of the growing seriousness of the Lutheran question and the widespread demand for closing ranks among loyal Catholics.

Most of his old liberal, humane friends in Italy and Rome were now dead. Of those who remained a number had been alienated from Erasmus, if not over religious issues, from one or another controversy, literary or scholarly quarrel, over the past twenty years. But perhaps most important, a new generation of critics and scholars now had the ear of the pope, a generation coming to maturity in the first round of the savage war of words and blows that the Reformation produced, and anticipating the intractable spirit of the Counter-Reformation.

One of these younger men was Alberto Pio, Prince of Carpi, a minor Italian noble and literary figure of distinguished lineage if somewhat modest accomplishment. His mother had been a sister of Pico della Mirandola and his tutor had been Erasmus's friend, the great Venetian scholar-printer Aldus Manutius. Erasmus had known Pio during his own stay, many years earlier, at the Aldine press. But now Pio was one of the leading figures of Rome's literary society; a familiar of Jerome Aleander, also a former friend of Erasmus from the days in Venice and now an important papal legate; and a friend of the papal secretaries Jacopo Sadoleto and Cardinal Pietro Bembo. Pio also had ties to France. He had been the ambassador in Rome of Louis XII and now of Francis I of France, and we may surmise that he was more fully informed than many others in Rome of the furor in France over Erasmus's writings and of the machinations of Erasmus's enemies in Paris to have his writings condemned.

In any event, Pio became the leading spokesman against Erasmus in Rome and busily spread the opinion that Erasmus not only subscribed to heretical Lutheran views but that he was the ultimate source from which Luther himself derived them. In 1526 Pio wrote a lengthy *Responsio* purporting to refute the heresies of Luther and openly asserting that many of them had come from Erasmus. The book was not immediately published. Pio, along with others, was forced to flee Rome when it was sacked by the imperial troops in 1527. He took up residence in France, under the patronage of the French king, where he continued his attacks upon Erasmus. In 1529 his *Responsio* was published by Bade in Paris, despite the best efforts of Erasmus to have it suppressed. Its charges were so serious and Pio himself of such influence that Erasmus felt obliged to respond and he hurriedly wrote a short tract that appeared, bound with some other items, in time for the spring Frankfort book fair of 1530 and thus gained wide circulation.

Erasmus, who had more than enough personal enemies among his critics, was particularly enraged by the gratuitous attack of Pio whom he had never really offended. This added to the bitterness of their quarrel, as did Pio's grim seriousness. Even at the time of his death some six months later, he was in the process of compiling twenty-three books of heresies and errors culled from Erasmus's writings. This work, again over Erasmus's protests, was published posthumously and again he felt obliged to respond.

In the meantime an issue related to the heretical charges against Erasmus had developed. Pio and other Italian literati had begun a campaign against Erasmus's literary and scholarly reputation. In part their criticisms were the same ones that other scholars and theologians had already leveled against his Greek New Testament. But his Italian critics now went beyond the substance of his scholarship to attack his style. To be accused of writing barbarous Latin was something he simply would not endure; indeed, one gains the impression that this wound to his literary vanity was more painful than the slurs on his scholarship or the charges against his orthodoxy. This attack was, moreover, part and parcel of the long-standing snobbery of the Italians, of their predilection to consider all non-Italians as barbarians, well-high incapable of writing a decent Latin. Erasmus had poked fun at them many times before, but now they were attacking him directly and personally. His response took the form of the *Ciceronianus*, a counterattack upon the literary affectations and neopaganism of his Italian critics.

The choice of title and subject derives from the leading literary

fashion in Rome at this time, called Ciceronianism. Reverence for Cicero as the greatest master of classical Latin prose had, of course, been a part of the humanist literary tradition since Petrarch and had passed on into the broader European Humanism of the early sixteenth century. Erasmus himself was a great admirer of Cicero. He had published editions of the *De Officiis* in 1501 and the *Tusculanae Quaestiones* in 1523, and his other works are filled with references to Cicero. But the Ciceronianism that Erasmus set out to attack in 1528 was a far different thing, an artificial, pedantic, affected pose which held that an acceptable Latin style was to be judged solely against the norm of Ciceronian Latin. The leading proponents of this affectation were the papal secretary Sadoleto and especially Cardinal Pietro Bembo, now the virtual dictator of Roman literary taste.

Erasmus's choice of subject was, however, not merely a target of convenience. Nor was it chosen entirely because of the personal slights of the Italian Ciceronians. To Erasmus the Latin language was the instrumentality that tied together the entire European community of letters, which, in its turn, offered the only hope for cosmopolitan learning, a common commitment to a reformed Christianity, and the hope for peace. The Latin language as he used it was a living language, rich, flexible, and vigorous. To have it turned into a dead language, forever limited to the Ciceronian vocabulary and syntax, unable to expand to new uses and new terminology, and of only antiquarian interest—this was the threat that formed the serious, even urgent basis for the *Ciceronianus*. Both Erasmus and the Ciceronians, of course, were betting against the future, as it turned out; which tends to make modern readers regard this controversy as trivial. But it was to its time and for its antagonists an issue fully as important as the related issues of religion.

The dialogue of *The Ciceronian* begins as Bulephorus ("Counsellor") and Hypologus ("Arbiter") see their friend Nosoponus ("Morbid Toiler") approaching, looking as pale and worn as a ghost. Bulephorus explains that he is suffering from a serious illness and suggests that they play along with him, pretend that they have suffered from the same ailment, and thus help him to recover. Nosoponus greets them and they commiserate with him on his illness. But what is it?, they inquire. And he answers that it is a burning desire to imitate the eloquence of Cicero. "Now I know your trouble," says Bulephorus, "you are seeking to gain that splendid and longed for name, Ciceronian."[14] Nosoponus agrees, "So much that I consider life bitter unless I attain it" (21). And, he goes on:

Not only the splendor of a most beautiful name torments me but also the insolent impertinence of those Italians, who, though they approve of no language at all except Ciceronian and think it the greatest disgrace for one not to be a Ciceronian, nevertheless declare that the honor of this name has never fallen to any on this side of the Alps. (22)

Even in the face of such discouragement, Nosoponus continues, he has persevered in his zeal to be a Ciceronian. He has touched nothing but Cicero's books for seven years. He has compiled three huge lexicons of Ciceronian vocabulary and usage that outweigh the entire collected works of Cicero. He will not even use the tense of a verb or the inflection of a noun not precisely found in Cicero. He has remained unmarried to avoid distraction and has shunned "public duty" and "ecclesiastical office" (29). Even the simplest letter— a note to a friend asking him to return some books he's borrowed— becomes a nightmare of composition and spoken Latin even a worse trial.

At this point, the problem defined, Bulephorus, with Hypologus's help, sets out to advise his friend. The long middle passage of the dialogue ensues and is a brilliant Socratic argument displaying not only Erasmus's linguistic good sense but his profound knowledge of both Cicero and the Ciceronian tradition.

The main elements of the argument are these.

Although it would seem desirable to emulate the best example in any undertaking, in this instance Cicero as the model of eloquence, note that even the ancients did not universally regard him as the best in every sort of rhetoric. Nor did they ever consider abandoning all the other excellent models of style and diction. Erasmus argues further that many of Cicero's works have perished but even if we had all his books there are subjects he did not handle. "If, therefore, we are compelled to speak on themes which he has not touched, where, pray, shall we seek a store of phrases?" (40). He continues: not only was Cicero sometimes careless and, by his own admission, made mistakes, but modern Cicero scholarship has so mutilated the texts that Cicero himself would hardly recognize them. He goes on to argue that Cicero perfected his own style from the wide study of others and if we slavishly imitate him alone we are like bad pupils who dishonor a good teacher. And, moreover, how can a barren imitation secure for us the kind of originality, the ingenuity of expression, the wisdom, the felicity, the power of persuasion that Cicero displayed. "If these are lacking, how indifferent will be our imitation" (54).

At this point Erasmus launches into his second theme of the dialogue. In order to speak well, he makes Bulephorus say, our language must be "consistent with the persons and conditions of present day life" (61). Cicero spoke of offices and institutions, of forms of government, gods and practices of religion long gone. But ". . . I stand on another stage, I see another theater, yes another world. What shall I do? I, a Christian, must speak to Christians about the Christian religion" (62). It is in this that the Ciceronians fail most significantly. Erasmus recalls, as he had in other places, an incident that occurred at the court of Julius II when he was in Rome and when a famous Roman orator—otherwise unnamed except that he "was no doubt a candidate for Ciceronianism" (63)— preached a sermon, supposedly on the death of Christ. Not only did he hail Julius II as Jupiter Optimus Maximus but he compared Christ to the Decii and Quintus Curtius and deplored his death as he might that of any "good and innocent man" such as Socrates. But there was "no mention of the secret plan of the omnipotent Father to redeem the human race from the tyranny of the devil by the unparalleled death of his only son nor of the mysteries—What it is to die with Christ, to be buried with him, with him to rise again" (64).

This was, of course, exactly how the current fad of Ciceronianism was applied to the matter of Christianity and Cardinal Bembo was famous for his classical sermons and orations, not so very different from the one Erasmus recalls. It is this charge of resurgent paganism that he levies against "the four Italians who recently have begun to boast themselves Ciceronians, though, as it has been shown, there is nothing more unlike Cicero than they" (86). They are not otherwise identified, but they could only be Bembo and the other chief figures of his circle.

This reference to "the four Italians" is the lead-in to what became the most controversial part of the dialogue. Bulephorus asks Nosoponus, "What Ciceronians can you mention to me, save only Cicero himself" (88). They begin with a listing of the ancient writers, and in a long *tour-de-force* passage, all of them are disqualified in one way or another as unworthy to be called Ciceronians.

Then, after the late Latin writers are reviewed, "let us come, if you please, to the Christians and see if we may find perchance some one who deserves to be called a Ciceronian" (91). And they go through the early Church Fathers and scholastics, again to no avail. They pass on "to another class of writers nearer to our own time"

(94), mainly the earlier Italian humanists—Petrarch, Boccaccio, Filelfo, Poggio, Valla, and the like and finally to the contemporary scene.

It is nearly impossible to avoid the conclusion that the chance to review his contemporaries was Erasmus's point in this whole elaborate exercise. It is equally hard to believe that he did not realize what a bombshell he was exploding. He had to know that, even though he put most of his judgments into the mouth of the silly and fatuous Nosoponus and even though the judgments strictly speaking were limited to Ciceronianism, it was inevitable that they would be regarded as his own and that they would be seen as judgments on the competence of his contemporaries as scholars and classicists. Despite the strictures of his Italian critics and others, Erasmus was still the most famous literary figure of his age and now at the height of his fame. Thus his literary judgments were bound to carry enormous weight. And if Erasmus's vanity was more wounded by literary slights than by charges of heresy, the same was true of his literary contemporaries.

Under these circumstances, it is hard to understand the list itself. One might expect him to use it to excoriate his Italian critics. And to an extent he does, at least with regard to Alberto Pio. But he makes no direct assault on the more important Ciceronians of Rome. Instead, he uses a curiously indirect device. A Flemish-French scholar named Christopher de Longueil, recently dead, had been involved with the Roman Ciceronian circle. Indeed, he may well have been the model for Erasmus's character Nosoponus. In any event Erasmus had no very exalted opinion of his literary accomplishments. This man, he contends, despite his failure to achieve the recognition he sought, came closer than any other this side of the Alps to being accepted by the haughty Ciceronians. The whole passage amounts to a condemnation of their taste as well as their judgment.

But it was a similar slight in his own list that brought down the harshest criticism upon Erasmus. The great French classicist and Greek scholar Guillaume Budé had never been on particularly good terms with Erasmus. He had never warmed to Erasmus's graceful overtures toward him and had bluntly criticized Erasmus on a score of things. Thus when Budé's name occurred in the list and the question was put, should he be regarded as a Ciceronian, the speaker is made to respond, "Why should I grant what he does not strive for and would not recognize if I should? Still, he deserves admiration for his great and varying gifts" (101). Rather cool praise for one whom many regarded as Erasmus's superior both as a scholar and a stylist. And to add to the slight, Budé was lodged beside Josse Bade, the Parisian printer-bookseller and sometime friend of Erasmus, who, while a respectable scholar, was surely not to be compared with Budé. Moreover, they were praised about equally. The friends of Budé, the adherents of the Roman Ciceronians—who persistently believed that Bembo was the model for Nosoponus—the champions of one after another of the men either ignored or slighted by this infamous listing, all attacked Erasmus in the years immediately following the publication of *The Ciceronian*. It turned out to be a more acrimonious controversy, more vicious and personal, than any he had ever been involved in—even the controversy with Luther was not so bitter. It pursued him to the end of his life and, try as he might, he was never able entirely to undo the damage.

CHAPTER 3

The Philosophy of Christ: Erasmus's Christian Scholarship and Devotional Works

O UR pursuit of Erasmus as a satirical writer has taken us many years and many miles beyond the cheerful London household of Thomas More, where Erasmus polished the final form of the *Praise of Folly* in the weeks following his return from Italy in the summer of 1509. The development of Erasmus as the greatest satirist of his age was, as we have seen, intimately related to the development of his religious thought. Indeed, that development is what gave point and purpose to his satirical writings. He himself emphasized the relationship between his obviously serious religious writings and the satirical purpose of such works as the *Praise of Folly* in the long and carefully reasoned letter he wrote to the Louvain theologian Martin van Dorp in the spring of 1515, defending the *Praise of Folly*. He noted that the ideas expressed in it were exactly the same as those presented in the *Enchiridion*.

His choice of the *Enchiridion* to bear the main burden of his comparison is significant. It had been written just at the turn of the century and was first published in 1503. In the subsequent decade or so Erasmus had come to regard it as the best example among his works of his "straightforward description of the Christian way of life."[1] Most modern critics agree. They further tend to regard it not only as among the clearest statements of his Philosophy of Christ, but as a bridge between the biblical scholarship that consumed most of the time and energy of Erasmus and accounts for the greatest bulk of his writings and the reform of Christian life that became his most compelling purpose.

We turn now to examine this important book.

57

I *The* Enchiridion Militis Christiani

The form and, to an extent, the content of the *Enchiridion* were shaped by the circumstances surrounding its composition. The title has an interesting double meaning, recalling Erasmus's love of ambiguity and of speaking *dupliciter*. The Greek word *enchiridion* means "something in the hand"—for such a bookish man as Erasmus, a manual or guidebook surely. But the rest of the title, *militis Christiani*, "of a Christian soldier," suggests the more militant reading "dagger" and in at least one later reference Erasmus uses the word *gladiolus*, "dagger," for it. From the first, however, he probably meant the reader to understand both meanings. For the book was written, he tells us, at the entreaty of a pious woman for her crude and philandering husband in the hope that it would help reform him. The husband—who was tactfully not identified in the text or dedication of the book—was probably Johann Poppenruyter, a friend of Erasmus whom he may have met through Jakob Batt's wide circle of contacts. Poppenruyter was a German cannon maker and soldier, who had recently established a foundry in Mechlin and who was later to achieve considerable fame for his armaments and be ennobled by the Archduke Charles. The wife appealed to Erasmus because, as he later recalled, her husband "had the greatest contempt for all theologians, only excepting me."[2] Erasmus, for his part, seems to have had a genuine fondness for Poppenruyter, enough so that he was willing—as he says at the end of the dedication letter—"to take a few days off" from his work in hand to write this book for him.

However willingly he undertook the task of writing the *Enchiridion*, the book he wrote in the autumn of 1501 was probably not the book he published two years later. We no longer have the manuscript presentation copy, but it was undoubtedly much shorter and less sophisticated than the first printed edition, probably very like several of his other brief letter-treatises that still survive.

The *exordium* ("opening argument") of the work is probably in much the same form as the original. It flows out of the dedicatory letter, referring to the request that Erasmus "prescribe in a concise fashion some method of living which might help you achieve a character acceptable to Christ,"[3] and immediately strikes a stern note of discipline, appropriate to the military vocation of the recipient. Erasmus indicates that he is glad enough to help, to comply with his friend's request, but that ". . . you must also exert yourself, lest you

seem to have asked my aid without a real reason or I to have complied with your wishes without real results" (37).

The argument moves immediately into the bristling military metaphor that frames the whole work. "Life is nothing but a kind of
perpetual warfare" (38). We are mistaken, Erasmus writes, we Christian soldiers, when, as the shock of battle ends and the physical conflict is over, we think the fighting is done. We sleep peacefully while
in reality "we are being assaulted without letup by such iron-shod
hordes of vices, ambushed by so many stratagems, beset by so many
snares" (38). We are under constant attack by demons against whom
the only defence is "the impenetrable shield of faith." Remember
that Erasmus interrupted his work on, and study of, the Pauline
Epistles to write the *Enchiridion* and that such imagery as Paul uses
in the sixth chapter of Ephesians, "the whole armor of God" including "the shield of faith," easily carried over to this writing. Likewise,
the Pauline notion of the inwardness of sin carries over into the next
passage.

> Then, as if so many enemies threatening us on all sides were not enough, within
> the most private recesses of our consciousness we carry a foe more intimate,
> more domesticated; and just as nothing in us is more secret, so nothing can be
> more dangerous. This is that ancient and earthly Adam. . . . We can neither
> wall him out nor drive him from our camp. This fellow we must watch with
> a hundred eyes or he may, perhaps, throw God's citadel open to the spirits of
> hell. (39)

Thus, the Christian soldier is never really at peace: what we mis-
take for peace is "actually the most shameful kind of war, for surely
a man who has come to terms with his vices has violated the covenant he made with God at his baptism" (39–40). That covenant of
baptism is the enlistment of the Christian soldier to his commander.
The sinner is thus a deserter, gone over to the enemy. Erasmus continues the military allegory. "In those insane wars that man wages
against man" (41) we risk our lives for our commander's praise or a
handful of empty symbols and then ignore the greater prize in God's
holy war against sin as we ignore the greater peril, the peril not of
death but of eternal damnation.

At the conclusion of the *exordium* he returns to the opening theme
of disciplined cooperation with God that will bring its reward, victory: "The outcome of your warfare . . . is not in doubt. In this

business no one has ever failed to win except the fellow who did not want to" (45).

Stripped to its essentials, as it is here, Erasmus has presented a simple, almost mechanistic view of operational Christianity, the sort of view a man of action could both understand and embrace. Man must exert himself and cooperate with God's will for his salvation. The enemy is both without and within—the assaults of Satan and the inward disposition to sin that in their turn cooperate to capture "God's citadel," the soul, and deprive man of his salvation.

The rest of the book is equally simple and straightforward and is essentially an outline of how the Christian soldier may proceed to accomplish his salvation and deny his enemies their victory over him. The directness shows in a number of ways. For instance, we do not find the familiar Erasmian style—sinuous, elegant, contrived, artfully careless and seemingly improvised. Rather, the *Enchiridion* marches on as straight and resolute as any Christian soldier. The structure of the book is a simple series of rules and remedies, partitioned and balanced, "this" offsetting "that." With chapter 9, for example, begins a sequence of "General Rules for the True Christian Life," for the art of living well has rules like anything else. These rules deal in part with the persons of God, Satan, and ourselves; in part with qualities such as vices and virtues. Twenty-two rules follow, including rules such as the second, "Action," "enter upon the way of spiritual health, not slowly or timorously, but resolutely" (87); the fourth, "Christ as the Only Goal," ". . . so that you may love nothing, marvel at nothing, want nothing but Christ or because of Christ" (95); or the nineteenth and twentieth, "Between God and Satan," "Between Virtue and Sin"—"the prizes are no less unequal than the prize-givers are unlike" (175).

The listing of rules for the Christian life gives way to a series of "Remedies for some Specific Sins." The list is conventional enough, including anger and vengeance, pride and swelling of the spirit, ambition, avarice; and the emphasis throughout is on manliness—"the only true honor proceeds from true virtue" (189), vengeance is womanly and contemptible. Erasmus observes that he has not attempted to deal with an elaborate catalog of sins, rather with a few examples that might be especially helpful to the one for whom the book is intended.

This kind of virile and uncomplicated Christian ethic was something that could be easily understood by such a man as Johann Poppenruyter. But there is no indication that he embraced it or that any other part of the "method of living" Erasmus prescribed had any effect on him. Many years later Erasmus sent his regards to "my old friend." He observed wryly that in exchange for the *Enchiridion* Poppenruyter had given him a dagger and that neither had made much use of the other's weapon!

But then, as we have already argued, the book that had been originally intended for this incorrigible soldier was rapidly changed, and the circumstances as well as the text of the first version became the pretext for a much more serious, much more personal work. For Erasmus took his own advice, to seek the inner man—and found that the Christian soldier of his title was really himself. Nor should such soul-searching introspection surprise us. Remember that, in the raw winter of 1500, he had returned from England to Paris, filled with resolution to turn to the serious study of Greek, Scripture, and the patristic sources of Christianity; and the image of John Colet was very much in his mind, stirring his own resolve to dedicate his life and studies to Christian ends.

He plunged into his work but was forced to leave Paris several times in search of patronage and to escape the plague. In 1501 he was in the Low Countries once more. It was at Tournehem, the residence of his friend Jakob Batt, tutor to the young Prince of Veere, that Erasmus agreed to write the *Enchiridion*. The presentation version was finished at St. Omer, where Erasmus was probably seeking the patronage of Antonius van Bergen, the Abbot of St. Bertin and the brother of his old patron the Bishop of Cambrai. But another monastic cleric of St. Omer was of far greater influence in the history of the *Enchiridion*, the prior of the Franciscan community there, Jean Vitrier, whom Erasmus came to know about this time. The influence of Vitrier strongly seconded that of Colet whom he resembled and with whom Erasmus always tended to link him in his own mind.[4]

Like Colet, Vitrier was a strong and somewhat ascetic personality who enjoyed a considerable reputation for purity of life. Like Colet, he had been attacked for his outspoken reform views: he was censured by the Sorbonne for his sermons on monastic abuse and the excesses of popular religion. Again like Colet, Vitrier was a passionate advocate of apostolic reform. He was fond of St. Paul and an avid student of the early church fathers—Erasmus mentions among them Ambrose, Cyprian, Jerome, and his special fondness for Origen. He also mentions that Vitrier was pleased even with the original version of the *Enchiridion*. It is likely, then, that the influence of Vitrier, the recollection of Colet, and the growing seriousness of his own religious and reform views combined to suggest to Erasmus the expansion of the *Enchiridion* into a more important and substantial work than it had been intended to be.

The first major shift occurs early in the book with chapter 3, "Concerning the Weapons of Christian Soldiering," a subject which should have grown directly out of the preceding opening exhortation to soldierly discipline. There are, he writes, two special weapons in the war of the spirit, prayer and knowledge, that work in support of each other. "Prayer . . . makes intercession; but knowledge suggests what ought to be prayed for" (47). Such weapons seem somewhat inappropriate to an unlettered soldier, and the long passage that follows is even more inappropriate. For it is clearly meant not for the Christian soldier but for the Christian scholar.

The weapon of prayer almost disappears from the discourse and it becomes a treatise upon Christian learning. Knowledge is most supportive of prayer, he begins, in "the eager study of sacred letters" (49). "If you will devote yourself earnestly to the study of Scripture, if you will ponder the law of the Lord both day and night, you will have no fear either by night or day, but be disciplined and trained against any onslaught of the adversary" (50).

This is followed by an even further departure from the original framework and purpose of the work:

As a matter of fact, for the early stages of this campaigning I would not disapprove of the new recruit's getting some practice in the works of pagan poets and philosophers: only let him take them up in moderation, in a way appropriate to his immaturity and, so to speak, in passing—without expending his life on them and rotting, as it were, on the crags of the Sirens. (50)

Surely this is not a hazard to which the ordinary soldier is exposed: Erasmus is speaking to himself and to others of like disposition. He continues, warning against adopting the bad moral habits of the ancients "as a result of studying their literature," but he notes also that there is much in them "conducive to right living." Moreover, "literature shapes and invigorates the youthful character and prepares one marvelously well for understanding Holy Scripture" (50–51). This is precisely the same argument, in capsule, that Erasmus will use time and time again in later life to defend his own scholarship and as the basis for much of his educational writing.

As understanding of Holy Scripture is prepared by classical studies, it is further buttressed by proper interpretation of Scripture itself. "From the interpretations of divine Scripture choose those which go as far as possible beyond literal meaning. After Paul, the best of the explicators of this sort are Origen, Ambrose, and Augustine" (53). As a corollary he scorns those "modern theologians"—he means scholastics—who spend their energies on "sophistical subtleties." The true understanding of Scripture is that Christ himself is the exemplification of all the things he taught, the essence of Scripture. If you are to understand Him—and you must do so to emulate Him—then you must understand Scripture, "let it permeate your whole being, let it be deeply and immovably fixed until there is not even an iota contained in Scripture that does not pertain to your spiritual well-being" (85). Again in capsule, this is Erasmus's entire methodology of Christian scholarship—the study of the pagan classics as an ethical base for Christian understanding, a turning to the sources of scriptural interpretation in the early church fathers, and a rejection of the "Thomists and Scotists," with the end being the understanding of Christ through the understanding of Scripture.

It is for this reason that Erasmus really objects to such things as the veneration of saints and the obsession with rituals. They can become an end in themselves—even as the love of classical study can—rather than a means to the true end of religion. We have already seen Erasmus inveighing against such externals of religion in his satirical works. He did so in the *Enchiridion* even earlier. Such criticism indeed is a prominent theme in this book, but, since it can only be tangentially related to the notion of the Christian soldier—especially as it trails off into a trenchant attack on monasticism—it is probably also a product of the revision of the original version.

Appearing in the midst of the recital of rules for the Christian life, in chapter 14 "From the Visible to the Invisible: the Way to a Pure and Spiritual Life," the subject suggests the contrast between the spiritual life and the veneration of saints. Erasmus is led to observe that the true veneration of saints is in the emulation of their faith. In the same vein he speaks of the relics of Christ:

Do you gape with awe at a robe or a handkerchief of Christ and then have trouble staying awake when you read what He said? You consider it vastly important to have at home a little fragment of the Cross, but that possession amounts to nothing in comparison to this other, that you carry the mystery of the cross deep within your heart. (112–13)

He goes on to speak of other externals of religion that lead the believer to miss the point. "Is it so very important," he asks, "that you make a physical trip to Jerusalem, when in your own heart there is a veritable Sodom, an Egypt, a Babylon?" (128). "Do not tell me . . . that Charity consists of frequent church attendance or genuflecting in front of the images of saints or burning candles or repeating a specified number of little prayers. God is not impressed by such routines" (122).

Even the sacraments, in and of themselves, without inward understanding, are useless. It is not so important to confess to a priest as to God, "for to confess before Him is to be inwardly penitent" (128). "If you are still wholly possessed by wrath, ambition, greed, lust, envy—then even if you are touching the very altar, you are still far from the sacrament" (110).

Erasmus was, of course, to express such views over and over again. And, as in his other writings the criticism of the externality of religious observances was closely tied to his criticism of monasticism, the same linkage was made in the *Enchiridion*. It was an easy connection to make as he spoke of the monks who think that daily repetition of the psalms is enough when they ignore the inner meaning. But there was more to be said on this favorite subject. He jabs at the uselessness of monks—as he would do in the *Colloquies* and the *Praise of Folly*—quite apart from their devotion (or lack of devotion) to their vows or their understanding of their own observances. He concludes this passage in the *Enchiridion* with the statement "Monasticism is not piety but a way of living, either useful or useless in proportion to one's moral and physical disposition" (198–99). This has been called the "most famous" sentence in the *Enchiridion*. It became the prime justification for the arguments of his critics condemning the book. As they observed, it was of a piece with his other criticisms of the monastic life. They failed to see (or to admit) that it was of a piece with his whole religious philosophy, that he condemned monasticism because by its very structure, routine, and observances it became a substitute for that inner spirituality that he considered "the law of the Gospel"; it diverted man from Christ.

This intense spiritualism, this inwardness of true religion is expressed throughout the *Enchiridion* to become its leading motif. And it is thoroughly Pauline. Indeed the *Enchiridion* is important as the first major document showing the developing Pauline basis for Erasmus's whole theology. The concept of sin that Erasmus evolves in the *Enchiridion* is a clear example of that development. In the original manuscript version of the book he balanced off an external concept of sin—"Satan" "the tempter," "attacking demons," and "iron-shod hordes of vices"—against an internal one, "that ancient and earthy Adam." But as in the case of the weapons of prayer and knowledge, the balance becomes unbalanced. As Erasmus refined, revised, and expanded his original work the balance swung from the external to the internal view: the battle is "between man and himself. Indeed, the battle array of the foe emerges from the depths of our own nature"[5] (62–63).

One of the most remarkable things about the *Enchiridion* is the extent to which it revealed the fundamental direction of Erasmus's Christian thought. Equally remarkable—when we consider the early date of this book, 1500–1503—is how fully it is developed. Roland H. Bainton has called the *Enchiridion* "programmatic,"[6] for in it we find virtually all the themes that will appear in Erasmus's later work—the need to differentiate between the real substance of religion and its empty forms, the importance of serious Christian scholarship in revealing the true nature of Christianity, and the imitation of Christ as the model of Christian behavior—in short, what Erasmus called his Philosophy of Christ.

The *Enchiridion* was not immediately successful. The first printed edition was published by Thierry Martens of Antwerp (1503), buried in an odd little collection of Erasmus's minor pieces. Its real celebrity began only with its publication as a single title, also by Martens, in 1515.

Some of its popularity was surely a matter of curiosity about this obviously different kind of book by the now celebrated author of the *Praise of Folly* who was, moreover, rapidly becoming a controversial figure in the world of learning and religion. Curiosity, however, cannot account for the fact that over the next twenty years more than thirty editions of the *Enchiridion* were published—including the handsome Froben edition of 1518 with a new preface by the author—and dozens more by the end of the century; nor can it account for the fact that it was translated in the course of the century into nearly every European language, in most cases in more than one version. Such a publication history can only be attributed to the substance of the book itself: it was its own best advertisement.

To an extent the *Enchiridion*'s popularity can be accounted for by the tremendous popular appetite for religious tracts that made such things the greatest staple of early printing. The *Enchiridion* is of the general type of lay devotional work that was already overwhelmingly popular. But the *Enchiridion* was different from such works as Thomas à Kempis's *Imitation of Christ*. Nowhere in it do we find the anguished theology of the cross or the vivid personalizing of either God or Satan that so terrified young Martin Luther. Books like *The Imitation of Christ* were essentially manuals of practical mysticism. The imitation of Christ that the *Enchiridion* advocated was the imitation of Christ's ethic. The *Enchiridion* was a manual of lay piety, not of lay mysticism. Earnest and troubled people at the turn of the sixteenth century were less concerned about what to believe or how to express it than they were about how to behave in a manner acceptable to other men and to Christ. The *Enchiridion* told them, in simple, uncomplicated terms, how to live by the philosophy of Christ as in ancient times men had lived by the philosophy of Plato, or Seneca, or Marcus Aurelius. And it told them so with no banter, no satire, no evasion, no stylistic tricks, and with a great moral earnestness. It had the appeal of a practical handbook.

Even the semifiction that the *Enchiridion* was a personal document intended for a specific individual lent it an intimate and appealing verisimilitude that worked well with its moral earnestness and evangelical tone. The universality of the idea of the Christian soldier added to its appeal and even though, as we have seen, the substantial additions Erasmus made in the revision of the original manuscript version strained the figure, it remained a kind of vivifying metaphor throughout. Even the book's advocacy of serious scholarly study and biblicism touched a popular chord. The humanists had done their work well and an increasing reading public was increasingly interested in reading the Bible and books about the Bible.

But indiscriminate Bible reading and the interest of laymen in biblical scholarship and criticism were not universally approved in the opening years of the sixteenth century. Many theologians and church officials viewed such enthusiasm with as much alarm as they viewed "irresponsible" criticism of the institutions of the church, not to mention church doctrine. And the *Enchiridion* offended in all these areas. Thus even such a generally blameless work as this came under suspicion. It had its champions, of course, and it had the silent approval of the vast numbers of people who read it. Erasmus would later note that the first edition was both "allowed" and "approved" by no less a personage than Adrian of Utrecht. But it had its critics too, who were increasingly sharp as the century progressed and bitter religious division led toward open religious war. The *Enchiridion*'s criticism of monasticism was reproved by Erasmus's English critic Edward Lee as early as 1518. His Spanish critics picked up on the same issue and objected as well to the statement that "Monasticism is not piety." Others objected to the book on the doctrinal grounds that it called into question aspects of the sacramental system, for example, confession, purgatory, indulgences. It was condemned by the Sorbonne along with the *Colloquies* as unfit to be read by students. Most of this criticism, like that of the *Colloquies*, was really an offshoot of the more serious charges stemming from Erasmus's work of Christian scholarship.

We turn now to examine that body of work.

II   *The Making of a Christian Scholar*

Erasmus's advocacy of a regimen of Christian scholarship in the *Enchiridion* was, as we have seen, a reflection of the program of study he was developing for himself. And it had started long before the *Enchiridion* was thought of. We have dealt at some length with Erasmus's struggle to become a humanist scholar, from the drills and exercises, the reading program and literary practice in the early years in the Brethren schools and the monastery, through the beginning of his serious study of Greek at the same time he wrote the *Enchiridion*, to the fame he had come to enjoy by the time the *Praise of Folly* was published in 1512.

Through those same years there were, in his books and letters, increasing references to the serious study of the ancient Christian classics, Scripture, and the church fathers. We have already noted his interest in Origen, Ambrose, and Augustine in the *Enchiridion*. But he had, already by this time, begun to develop a special fondness for St. Jerome. As early as the years at Steyn he claimed to have written out as many of Jerome's letters as were available to him. In the winter of 1500 he expressed the need for the whole works of Jerome "upon whom I am preparing commentaries."[7] In another letter of about the same time he wrote, "I have long ardently wished to illustrate with a commentary the Epistles of St. Jerome, and in daring to conceive so great a design, which no one has hitherto attempted, my heart is inflamed and directed by some divine power."[8]

Within another year he had turned to Scripture and, probably with the example of Colet before him, to the letters of St. Paul. He later told Colet that at that time he was writing something on the Epistle to the Romans (likely a commentary).

Then, in the late autumn of 1504, he discovered apparently quite by accident in a monastery outside Louvain a manuscript copy of Lorenzo Valla's *Notes on the New Testament.* He took the manuscript with him when he returned to Paris a few months later and, with the encouragement of friends, decided to edit and publish the work. By midwinter he had arranged for its printing with Josse Bade under the title *In Latinam Novi Testamenti interpretationem ex collatione Graecorum exemplarium Adnotationes,* which would be the first printed edition of this hitherto almost unknown work. Valla had always been among Erasmus's favorite "moderns." But, prior to his discovery of the manuscript of the *Adnotationes,* he evidently knew of Valla's biblical scholarship only indirectly if at all. That discovery, coming as it did at this crucial time in Erasmus's own development as a Christian scholar, was to be perhaps the most important link to his eventual resolution to produce his edition of the Greek New Testament, in a sense to complete the work that Valla had so well begun. For Erasmus was now able to see how revolutionary Valla's work was, the first instance of the new, humanistic philology, applied to Scripture.[9]

Through the year 1505 Erasmus's biblical scholarship continued at an increasing pace, in Paris and especially in London, where he went once more toward the end of the year. Busy as he was, scrambling for preferment and distracted by a host of projects, he nevertheless was able to undertake an even greater and more audacious task than his "correction" of St. Jerome—his "correction" of the New Testament itself. His work took the form of an entirely new, fresh Latin translation of the text, excepting Acts and Revelation, along with some introductory commentary on the Epistles. We may probably look once more to the influence of Colet in this work. He was now Dean of St. Paul's in London and lent Erasmus Greek and Latin manuscripts for his collation from the cathedral and school libraries. It was Colet, moreover, who had the translations copied out after Erasmus left for Italy. But by this time Erasmus's Christian scholarship had a life of its own, mature and substantially free of external influences—even the influence of Colet—and was rapidly developing toward the great publication projects of the next decade.

Erasmus's stay in Italy was, as we have seen, largely occupied with more secular concerns led by the great Aldine edition of the *Adagia,* which, more than any previous work, established his reputation as a scholar. But Italy also showed him the cynicism, venality, and wholesale corruption of the Italian clergy and, perhaps most important, the brutal secularism of the papacy personified in Pope Julius II. This bundle of impressions completed the preparation of Erasmus the satirist. But, as we have seen, his satirical genius ultimately rested upon his convictions as a reformer of the church and a Christian scholar. In this sense the visit to Italy had a strong and positive effect in turning him back, even more seriously, to the work he had left behind in England.

He returned to England in the summer of 1509, but, as we have seen, his expectations of royal patronage from the young scholar-king Henry VIII failed to materialize and in the summer or fall of 1511 Erasmus was constrained to accept the Lady Margaret Professorship of divinity at Cambridge, the same appointment he had abandoned to go to Italy. Although the appointment carried some prestige and a reasonable living, Erasmus was from the first only tolerably content at Cambridge. He never cared much for university life, even at its best; and Cambridge was remote and provincial. He still cherished hopes of patronage and looked constantly toward London where those hopes lay and where most of his friends still were.

His letters from Cambridge are full of petty complaints—he was often ill and complained of the local beer; he complained even more bitterly when a cask of Greek wine sent by Ammonio was broken into by the carters, half drunk and the other half spoiled. Some of his fellow scholars at Queens' were congenial spirits and a few remained firm friends. But on the whole he dismissed them contemptuously as "Thomists and Scotists" or, as he wrote to his gossipy friend Ammonio, "nothing but Cyprian-bulls and dung eaters [while] they think they are the only persons that *feed on ambrosia and Jupiter's brain!*"[10] He could not find a copyist who could even write tolerably—"What a University!"[11] Again later he wrote to Ammonio, "There is a great solitude here, most people away for fear of the plague, though when all are here it is still a solitude."[12]

As often as he could he slipped away to London. But the plague—more virulent there than in Cambridge—his own health, his work, and his poverty kept him away from the city for months at a time. His financial difficulties were especially annoying, and what hope remained of royal patronage was put beyond his reach by Henry VIII's increasing occupation with foreign politics, followed in the summer of 1513 by his invasion of France in alliance with the Emperor Maximilian. Erasmus had already importuned his friends so often that they avoided him; there was even a sharp exchange or two with Colet over the subject of money. Others of his friends, especially those close to the court, were deeply engaged in Henry's foreign adventure. Erasmus's old friend Mountjoy was the governor of some occupied strong points along the Flemish-French frontier. Still others were heavily obligated for special levies demanded by the war. In the spring of 1512 Archbishop Warham had finally settled upon Erasmus a pension derived from the income of a rectory in Kent and, about the same time, Mountjoy had arranged for an annual pension for him. These would eventually become substantial, but at this time the income was small from both sources and not regularly paid because of the war. Moreover, there were misunderstandings over the arrangements for his compensation at Queens'.

But with all its vexations and disappointments, this period of time, particularly the time at Cambridge, was among the most productive periods of his life. As we have already seen, he wrote the *Julius exclusus* during this time. But it was no more than a diversion from more serious work. He was engaged once more on a still larger edition of the *Adagia* and much concerned with the plans for its publication. He worked intermittently on a book he had promised for Colet's school, the *De Copia*. He was preparing an edition of Seneca and continued his translations from Greek, "a good many books of Plutarch," some more of Lucian's dialogues, and the Greek fathers Basil and Chrysostom.

But his principal occupation throughout all this time at Cambridge was his work on St. Jerome and the New Testament. As we have seen, he had prepared an almost complete translation of the New Testament before leaving for Italy and Colet had had it copied. Erasmus picked up this work once more at Cambridge, correcting and revising it. His letters are full of references to it. In the fall of 1512 he wrote his friend Peter Gillis in Antwerp that he had completed the correction of the entire New Testament. Within the next year, perhaps sooner, he turned to the task of collecting as many manuscripts as he could find—we can identify four Greek manuscripts he used at Cambridge and there were probably others, both Greek and Latin—to produce a new edition of the Greek New Testament, with his own notes added in the manner of Valla's annotations.[13]

At the end of the first week in July, 1514, Erasmus left England, and from the Castle of Hamme in Flanders, where he had stopped to visit Mountjoy, the governor of the castle, he wrote his prior, Servatius Rogerus, "I'm now on my way to Germany, to Basel to be exact, to publish my works."[14] This decision was to lead him into association with the printing firm of Froben and Amerbach and the most important publishing venture of his career.

III   *Basel and the Froben Press*

It had begun quite accidentally and with some suspicion and annoyance. Before leaving England Erasmus had, for some reason, entrusted a bundle of manuscripts including a new edition of the *Adagia* to a publishers' agent and bookseller named Franz Birckman in Antwerp with instructions to deliver them to Josse Bade in Paris, with whom arrangements for their printing had already been made. Instead, Birckman delivered them to Johann Froben in Basel, for whom he also worked on commission. By the time Erasmus learned of the deception there was little he could do but make a virtue of necessity. It was for this reason that he was on his way to Basel "to publish my works."

Erasmus may not have been as outraged as he pretended to be. After all, what Froben had done was by no means unheard of in the cut-throat business of early commercial printing[15] and the Froben-Amerbach Press was a well-established house with a good reputation. Froben, moreover, had Greek type and knew how to use it. Only a year before he had printed a pirated edition of the Aldine *Adagia* that elicited a grudging admiration even from Erasmus.

Another matter may also have influenced Erasmus's decision. For some years the Froben-Amerbach Press had been engaged in printing critical editions of the "Doctors of the Latin Church." St. Ambrose had appeared in 1492, Augustine in 1506. And Erasmus may well have been aware that a massive edition of St. Jerome was under way. Erasmus's later friend Beatus Rhenanus actually says that it was the knowledge of the Jerome edition that brought him to Basel. Erasmus had devoted too many years to his own work on Jerome to allow him to be printed without his participation in the project if there were any way to "get in on" it.

Thus, for whatever reason and in whatever temper, Erasmus pressed on to Basel, arriving there in August of 1514, and sought out Froben. On their first meeting he presented himself jokingly not as Erasmus but as a friend of Erasmus authorized to deal for him and so like him "that whoever sees me, sees Erasmus." Froben immediately saw through this puckish trick, insisted that Erasmus stay with him, had his baggage brought from the inn where he had lodged, and welcomed him to his home, his shop, and his circle of friends, co-workers, and employees.

It was the story all over again of Erasmus's introduction to the household of Aldus. The circle of men gathered at the Froben Press indeed resembled the Aldine Academy. Some of them were simply learned friends of Froben or the Amerbachs, rather casually related to the work of the press, like Ludwig Bär, the rector of the University of Basel and an old family friend of the Amerbachs; the eminent lawyer and imperial councillor Ulrich Zäsi of nearby Freiburg; or Wilhelm Kopp, already a longtime friend of Erasmus and royal physician to Louis XII of France who often returned to his home in Basel. Others worked for the press. Some of these were already established scholars. The great Hellenist and Hebrew scholar Johann Reuchlin had been attracted by the Jerome project and had worked for the press, correcting the text of Jerome in 1510. And, of course, there were the Amerbach brothers, Bruno and Basil, learned in Latin, Greek, and Hebrew, and the younger brother Boniface, a student of law under Zäsi. And there were others who drifted in and out of the shop and household.

Any doubts Erasmus might have had or any reservations he had brought with him about Froben or the Froben Press quickly vanished. The hospitality of the Froben circle, the warmth and friendship of Froben himself, and the adulation with which Erasmus was received made him at home. He was invited immediately to take part in the completion of the Jerome project—as he had hoped. He was back once more in his favorite milieu—amid the clatter and noise of the press, with printers and pressmen working about him, surrounded by manuscripts, books, galleys, secretaries, proofreaders, editors, correctors, and copy-boys. He threw himself eagerly into the work. And there was much work to be done. He had promised to revise the *De Copia* for Colet and was committed to a book of instruction for the Archduke Charles, the later *Institutio Principis Christiani*. There was also the project of reprinting the *Enchiridion*. The books that Birckman had taken to Froben were started, the

Plutarch pieces, the edition of Seneca, and the new *Adagia*. But these projects were now distinctly secondary to the great project of completing the Jerome edition. The format of the work was already established and the printing well advanced. Erasmus claimed the volumes of letters as his special responsibility. The text of the letters was largely complete by this time and he turned to finishing the marginal notes and adding new annotations and arguments. But because of his lifetime of work on Jerome he quickly became, in effect, the senior editor of the project and was consulted about the collation of manuscripts, variant readings, questions of fact.

But even as he plunged into the work on Jerome, he and Froben had already come to an agreement on Erasmus's other great project, the Greek New Testament. Before the end of September the project had been outlined: Erasmus mentions not only an annotated Greek text but "a me versum," a reference clearly to his own translation.

Erasmus was eager to get on with the project, Froben possibly even more so. The great age of biblical scholarship was obviously at hand. Aldus had begun to produce an Old Testament in Hebrew, Greek, and Latin in 1501, but the project was never completed— Pope Adrian VI would later urge Erasmus to undertake it. The French scholar LeFevre had already done a critical edition of the Psalms, the so-called *Quintuplex Psalter* (from the five versions printed in parallel columns) in 1509 and in 1512 a critical Latin text of St. Paul's Epistles. More formidable was a massive project being done at the Spanish University of Alcalá, under the patronage of the great Cardinal-Archbishop Ximenes de Cisneros, to produce a definitive multilingual text of the entire Bible. It was thus called the *Complutensian Polyglot* (*Complutum* was the Latin name for Alcalá). It contained Hebrew, Greek, and Latin texts of the Old Testament and Greek and Latin texts of the New Testament. The New Testament was complete, set in type and ready to be printed, delayed only by the cardinal's insistence upon waiting for the pope's *imprimatur*. As it turned out it was further delayed by the cardinal's death in 1517 and did not appear until 1520. Froben may not have known how close the *Complutensian* was to publication, but he knew it was close. The immense and costly volume of Erasmus's New Testament had to be published first!

The resulting sense of urgency permeated the whole project and affected every aspect of the work, even carrying over to the work on the Jerome, although that work was much nearer completion. Erasmus had already accumulated a mass of notes on the text of the letters, explaining obscure points and noting corrupt or interpolated passages, and set the letters in chronological order. But he still had to check his readings against the collection of manuscripts that the editors of the Amerbach project had been using and reconcile differences—a long, meticulous, and tedious job—for there was simply no reliable textual tradition for Jerome. And, of course, this involved further annotation. For the final version, parts of the text had to be restored, often Greek and Hebrew passages that had been lost or corrupted in transmission. For the Hebrew he was fortunate to have the help of the other scholars assembled at the press, the Amerbach brothers in particular and later, for the New Testament, Joannes Oecolampadius (Johann Hussgen), still later to be the reformer of Basel. Erasmus confessed himself, "I make no claim to Hebrew, which I have only tasted with the tip of my tongue." But whether the corrections were of Hebrew, Greek, or Latin passages or the annotations by his own hand or others, the various readings were scrupulously assembled by Erasmus in a separate volume for scholars' comparison.

There was much more work to be done on the New Testament and much greater pressure of time. Erasmus had expected to find good Greek manuscripts of the New Testament in Basel that would provide a basis for the printed version with a minimum of correction. But this was not the case. The five manuscripts available to him were all faulty, extremely disparate, and requiring a vast amount of work to produce a coherent text for the printing. The best of the lot had been taken off by Reuchlin and had to be borrowed back from him. But none of the manuscripts contained the Book of Revelation. Reuchlin was persuaded to lend another manuscript for the work that did contain the Revelation text. It was very old: Erasmus thought it dated from apostolic times though it now appears to be no earlier than the twelfth century. But even here the text of Revelation was badly muddled and intermixed with commentary so that Erasmus was forced to copy out the text for the correctors to use. And the last five verses or so were missing, even in the Reuchlin manuscript. Erasmus decided to retranslate them from the Latin into Greek, a fact that he clearly noted in his apparatus.

At the same time, the scope of the work was growing. The annotations to the Greek text were originally conceived as rather perfunctory, but as the differences from the Vulgate increased, so did the notes, from a proposed thirty sheets to more than eighty. In addition, it was proposed to publish a new translation by Erasmus. In the spring of 1515 he made another hurried visit to England, possibly to get the translation he had earlier completed at Cambridge. As it turned out, however, this translation was not used in the first edition because it was decided that it varied too much from the Vulgate, although Erasmus himself preferred it and had confidence in its validity.

Back in Basel through the summer and fall of 1515 the work continued at a furious pace, Erasmus working, as he wrote, "standing on one foot"—the sheets pouring from his desk one after another with only a correction or two to the page and often getting ahead of the correctors and proofreaders. The work—both the New Testament and the Jerome—was not so much being published as "tumbling out of the press."

Even before the printing had begun the news, especially of the Greek New Testament, had attracted critics. Erasmus needed to protect himself and his work as it neared completion. His first thought had apparently been to dedicate both the New Testament and the Jerome to his old patron Archbishop Warham. But shortly after arriving in England, on his quick trip there in the summer of 1515, he was already considering dedicating the work instead to Pope Leo X. In particular he was thinking of the St. Jerome since it seemed likely that, of the two projects, it would appear first. He may indeed have come to England in part to mend his fences with the archbishop and to solicit his own contacts there with the papal court. He was evidently reassured. On May 15, he wrote to Cardinal Riario, the best of his old friends in Rome and still a powerful figure in the papacy, asking his advice, sounding him out whether he should dedicate the book to Leo. After all, he wrote, it would be singularly appropriate for "the prince of all theologians" to be dedicated to "the prince of all popes." At the same time he wrote to Cardinal Grimani in the same vein. And then, on May 21, he addressed Leo directly. He had, of course, known him also in Rome as Giovanni Cardinal dei Medici though not as well as either Grimani or Riario. It was a long, flattering and elegant letter that finally got to the point: might he hope that the St. Jerome would be permitted to appear under his auspices and with his commendation? Six weeks later the response from Leo came, "under the seal of the fisherman," in the hand of the papal secretary Sadoleto and in his formal hieratic Latin. The pope will not only approve the dedication, he will consider it "the greatest possible gift" and await it eagerly.[16]

It was not, however, the Jerome that appeared first. Paper shortages held up that massive, multivolume work. It was the fascicles of the New Testament—Erasmus chose to borrow St. Jerome's preferred term and call it *Novum Instrumentum*—that began to come off the press in December, 1515, the notes first with a preface addressed "To the Pious Reader," the text itself appearing a few weeks later with a dedicatory preface to Pope Leo X, dated February 1, 1516. Erasmus was presuming upon the good will of the pope for which he had some assurance in their earlier exchange over the Jerome as well as that of such friends as Ammonio, who assured him of Leo's favor. Leo's brief containing his enthusiastic and unqualified endorsement of the New Testament was delayed, however, and reached Erasmus only in 1518, in time to be printed in the front matter of the second edition, and with every later edition during Erasmus's lifetime.

For better or worse, the New Testament was done, the colophon dated in March, 1516, and the work running to more than a thousand folio pages. And St. Jerome was not far behind. On March 17, Erasmus wrote to one friend, "The New Testament is published; and the last page of Jerome is being finished;"[17] to another on May 12, "The New Testament is finished somehow, Jerome stands panting at the winning-post, and will presently be in the hands of the public."[18] The New Testament was, by this time, for sale in Paris and at the spring Frankfort book fair.

The Jerome was published that same spring, in nine heavy volumes, the first four being Erasmus's edition of the letters, with separate volume prefaces dated from January to March, and a dedicatory preface to the entire work, dated April 1, 1516, and addressed not to Pope Leo but to Erasmus's faithful and patient patron Archbishop Warham.

IV   *"The Golden Year"*

The work of half a lifetime had culminated for Erasmus in that spring of 1516, and he stood at the pinnacle of his fame. Ammonio wrote from England, "You have found the way to immortality. All honor to your genius!"[19] And Pirckheimer from Nürnberg, "You have secured your name against the assaults of time, and completed a performance not less acceptable to Almighty God than useful and necessary to all faithful servants of Christ."[20] Thomas More was enthusiastic, as was Colet, who finally admitted that he now wished he had learned Greek "without a knowledge of which we are nothing."[21] We have already noted the approval of the Jerome that came from Leo X, and his endorsement of the Greek New Testament was to come shortly. In all Erasmus was so showered with testimonials that even he was embarrassed by them. The incredible volume of work Erasmus had done in the past year and a half was impressive enough. But more than the brute mass of the work itself, its conception, its organization, and its approach to the problems of substance and interpretation may be said to mark the beginning of modern scriptural and patristic scholarship.

Erasmus was more pleased with the Jerome than with the New Testament, and with some justification. It was a more meticulous work done over a longer time, both with more deliberation and with better and more abundant sources. In the editing of the letters he strove to recover the authentic text and, as we have noted, scrupulously catalogued variant readings. He provided notes to the text which are among the earliest instances of modern critical apparatus in that they form a tissue of continuous commentary on the text— not the traditional scholastic scholia of interpretation, but rather historical and philological commentary. This is not to say that Erasmus avoided substantive comment. Quite the contrary: he entered much more directly and personally into the notes than is now fashionable. They often became little homilies in the manner of his comments in the *Adagia*. When, for example, he encounters a passage in which Jerome is exhorting his reader to Christian poverty, Erasmus finds an excuse for excoriating the fiscality and secularism of the contemporary church establishment.

Although Erasmus had worked from time to time on various of the church fathers, including Jerome, the great Froben edition of 1516 was his first major publication of a patristic text. And he continued, in one way or another, to labor on Jerome all the rest of his life. The 1516 text was revised, corrected, and reissued in 1521. A further revision was done in 1524 and a definitive new edition in 1526. Another edition was published in Paris in 1533–34, and another Froben edition, part of the projected Erasmus *Opera*, was published after Erasmus's death, in 1536–37. In addition to this continuing work on Jerome, in 1519 he published his edition of St. Cyprian, in 1522 Arnobius, in 1523 St. Hilary. In 1524 appeared his commentary on two hymns of Prudentius. In 1525 he published his translation of some of the tracts of St. John Chrysostom and expressed the intention of doing the entire *Opera*. In 1526 appeared the *Opus* of Irenaeus and in the following year some of the minor works of Athanasius. He had begun, probably as early as 1523, to work on a new edition of St. Ambrose, based on the Amerbach edition of 1492. This work he completed in four volumes in 1527 and two years later published two more treatises of Ambrose hitherto unknown, which he had found in manuscript. Froben had proposed in 1517 that Erasmus revise the earlier Amerbach edition of St. Augustine. But he found the work very faulty and began instead a substantially new edition on which he worked intermittently until 1529 when his edition of the Augustine *Opera* appeared in ten volumes. In 1530 he finally collected the scattered editions of the various works of Chrysostom he had done over several years and published the *Opera*. In 1532 appeared his St. Basil, in 1533 Haymo. Thirty years earlier he had begun to edit the fragments of Origen's work. He had published an edition of Origen in 1527 and had almost finished the revision of this work at the time of his death: it was published immediately afterward.

So substantial was this work of editing patristic texts—some thirty folio volumes, not counting the several editions and revisions of various works—and so influential his method and approach that he became the leading force in bringing about what one scholar has called a "patristic Renaissance."[22] Another has observed that "he not only laid the foundations of critical patristic studies, but directed theological interest away from the medieval schoolmen."[23]

For all the profound effect of the St. Jerome and the massive patristic editions that followed it, Erasmus's New Testament was more significant. It was the first Greek text of the New Testament ever published, a systematic attempt to recover the very words in which it was originally written. It was, moreover,—in its carefully restored text, translation, and notes—the first great tool of modern biblical scholarship. The text was not to be much improved until the biblical criticism of the nineteenth century. The notes, learned as they were, tended not to be terribly formidable. On the contrary they were easy to read, anecdotal, and filled with Erasmus's customary comments on the current scene.

Yet, for all its significance, the first edition of the *Novum Instrumentum* was faulty—hastily printed, filled with errors, and based upon inadequate manuscript sources. Erasmus knew it, was dissatisfied with it, and began immediately preparing for a new edition. He wrote to Pirckheimer in November of 1517 that he hoped it would be finished within four months. But that was far too optimistic: there was too much to be done. He completely revised the Greek text from more than half a dozen additional manuscripts. For the translation he returned in every detail to the preferred earlier version he had made at Cambridge, in spite of its far greater divergence from the standard Vulgate text. The notes and commentaries were much sharper in their criticism of clergy and of ecclesiastical abuses, including indulgences, and the position of the church on divorce. And they raised the suspiciously Donatist question of the Christian's obligation to obey unworthy church officials. In March of 1519 the new edition was published by Froben, the title changed to the more usual *Novum Testamentum*, which it retained in all subsequent editions.

Further revisions were made from still other manuscripts, from readings supplied by friends and critics alike, even from the Complutensian Bible, a copy of which he had by 1522—through further editions of 1522, 1527, and 1535, all printed by Froben and going through no less than sixty-nine printings in Erasmus's lifetime.

V *The Paraphrases, the Bible, and "the Christian Man"*

Even before the first edition of the New Testament was published Erasmus had conceived and perhaps even begun a related project, a series of paraphrases of the New Testament books. The first of these, the paraphrase of Romans, was published by Thierry Martens in Louvain in 1517 and reprinted by Froben in 1518. In the same year Erasmus noted in a letter that he was resuming work on the project and that by the winter of 1519 he hoped to be finished with the paraphrases of all the Epistles shortly. Instead, apparently, he turned to the Gospels. The paraphrase of Matthew was published in 1522, the other three in 1523. Each was dedicated to one of the great contemporary kings—Matthew to Charles V, John to Charles's brother Ferdinand, Mark to Francis I, and Luke to Henry VIII. The paraphrase of the Acts of the Apostles was published in 1524 and dedicated to Pope Clement VII. The paraphrases of the remaining epistles followed through the rest of the decade.

Erasmus considered these paraphrases more widely useful even than the New Testament; in a sense they were a popularization of that more scholarly work meant to simplify and explain Scripture. Although the paraphrases, like the notes to the New Testament, were based upon the ancient patristic commentators, they were essentially Erasmus himself, recasting, retelling, and reinterpreting the familiar matter of the New Testament. His friend Beatus Rhenanus reported his comment, "Here I am on my own field of action."[24]

His framework of interpretation was not radically innovative—remember that he was preparing a popularization. His principal theme, like that of his other popular religious writings, was the Philosophy of Christ, the conviction that Scripture is to be understood as an exhortation to Christlike conduct. His explication of the Mary and Martha story, for example, stressed that there is room for a variety of ways to serve Christ. In the parable of the prodigal son, he concluded, "Now in the natural love of this father for his son behold the goodness of God, who is far more clement to sinful man, if only he repent and despise himself, than any father toward his son, however tenderly he may love him."[25]

But Christlike behavior depends not only on the willingness of man so to behave, but on his willingness to put his faith in Christ. In his homily on the miracle of the loaves and fishes, Erasmus wrote: "Whatever you have, place it in the hands of Jesus. Let him bless and break it and give it to you. Then you will give it to the people, not as your own but as coming from Him."[26]

In another instance, he asked how it was that those who believed in Christ were cured of diseases by touching the hem of his garment, whereas those who handled his body to scourge and execute him were not affected. And his answer was that the faith with which they touched Him was the important thing, not the touching itself. Such insistence upon faith sounded alarmingly Lutheran in the decade of the 1520s and gave a further handle to Erasmus's critics.

But neither the suspicion of Lutheran leanings nor any other strictures of his enemies affected the popularity of the paraphrases. He had hoped they would be popular, for he wanted to see the Bible and the understanding of Scripture available to everyone including, as he wrote in the preface to the paraphrase of Matthew, "the farmer, the tailor, the mason, prostitutes, pimps, and Turks." The paraphrases were successful beyond his expectations. They went through edition after edition in the Latin version. They were quickly translated into French, German, Bohemian, and English. In 1547, at the beginning of the Protestant reign of young Edward VI of England, it was decreed that the English translation of the paraphrases be set up in every church along with the English Bible. Thus the paraphrases became part of the whole complex movement that tied "the word of God" so securely to the emerging Protestantism of Europe and saw the translation of the Bible into virtually every European tongue.

Fully as much as for the paraphrases, Erasmus cherished the hope that his New Testament would find its way into the hands of every person capable of reading it. In the preface to the volume of notes, addressed "To the Pious Reader," he wrote: "We are engaged in a holy occupation, and in one which commends itself to the world by its special purity and simplicity. . . . In simple and pure zeal we are furnishing these Scriptures for Christian hearing so that in future more may make use of this sacrosanct philosophy."[27] He meant, of course, the Philosophy of Christ.

At no place in his writings did Erasmus more explicitly spell out the relationship he sought to establish between sacred scholarship and the Christian vocation than in one of the several prefaces he prepared for the first edition of the New Testament. He called it *Paraclesis*, which in Greek means a summons or exhortation. The obvious reference is to the Holy Spirit, the comforter promised his disciples by Christ. But Erasmus made it a call for the Christian to study Holy Scripture—as he had called the reader of the *Enchiridion* to do—where alone he will find the teachings of Christ, the guide and comforter for his own individual life.

It is neither a long nor complex argument. The Philosophy of Christ, he argues, is not like other philosophies, demanding "that you approach equipped with so many troublesome sciences. The journey is simple, and it is ready for anyone. Only bring a pious and open mind, possessed above all with a pure and simple faith."[28]

The Philosophy of Christ is available to all levels of sophistication and appropriate to all people whatever their age, sex, fortune, or position in life. For that reason, he continues, "I disagree very much with those who are unwilling that Holy Scripture, translated into the vulgar tongue, be read by the uneducated" (97). And then comes this famous lyrical passage:

I would that even the lowliest woman read the Gospels and the Pauline Epistles. And I would that they were translated into all languages so that they could be read and understood not only by Scots and Irish but also by Turks and

Saracens. . . . Would that, as a result, the farmer sing some portions of them at the plow, the weaver hum some parts of them to the movement of his shuttle, the traveler lighten the weariness of the journey with stories of this kind. (97)

Just as the truth of Christ should be available to all men, all men can be theologians, and those who can best teach the truth of Christ are those who exemplify it in their lives, even if they be "a common laborer or a weaver." It was an assertion perilously close to the Lutheran notions of vocation and the priesthood of all believers, as Erasmus's critics would be quick to point out. But Erasmus here is not a disputant. He is seeking to be a peacemaker. If the doctrines of Christ were universally known, "Christendom would not be so disturbed on all sides by almost continuous war," "noisy disputation" would cease, and "we would not differ from those who do not profess the philosophy of Christ merely in name and ceremonial" (99).

It must strike us as anomalous that, on the one hand, Erasmus called so passionately for Holy Scripture to be in the hands of women, children, laborers, prostitutes, pimps, Turks, and Irishmen, and yet, on the other, he prepared a text of Scripture that was clearly a scholar's book. Except to a degree, for the paraphrases, Erasmus's biblical scholarship was closed to the very masses of people he hoped to address. The direct relationship he sought between that scholarship and popular religion was an impossible goal, both because of the level of sophistication of his scholarship and more importantly because he was himself unable to put it into the peoples' languages. He was dependent upon translations to reach them, and, as we have seen, he enthusiastically endorsed the vernacular translation of Scripture. With equal enthusiasm he advocated the extension and improvement of humanist education. But this was no more than a partial measure. For Erasmus himself could never conceive such education as available to farmers and weavers or generally to the children of "the people."

Thus, between his calling as a scholar and his goal as a reformer there was a discontinuity he was never able to reconcile. The master of paradox was himself caught in a paradox he could not resolve. And in his better moments he knew it. He was condemned by his own choices to a position at one remove from the audience he hoped to reach, to be the theologian's theologian, to prepare the tools with which others would work to bring Christ to the people. Important as this role was it was never entirely satisfactory. For he could not dictate the inferences others would draw from his work, much less the uses to which they would put it. It is instructive to note that both Luther and Tyndale based their translations of the New Testament upon Erasmus's *Novum Testamentum*.

CHAPTER 4

"The Egg that Luther Hatched": Erasmus's Controversial Writings

THE publication of the Jerome and the Greek New Testament capped Erasmus's career as a Christian scholar. The famous, the interested, the curious wrote him letters hoping for a reply, no matter how perfunctory. He was sought after and invited everywhere. The Duke of Bavaria pressed him to accept a well-paid professorship at Ingolstadt. A similar invitation to Leipzig came from the ruler of Ducal Saxony. Francis I invited him to come to Paris and promised a stipend of a thousand francs a year. Cardinal Ximenes invited him to come to Spain. His name was proposed for the post of Public Orator in Venice. His highly placed friends in Rome urged him to return there, and the favor of Pope Leo X made such a move a powerful temptation.

But, early in 1516, Erasmus was appointed a councillor to the Archduke Charles, the lord of the Burgundian Netherlands, whom Erasmus regarded as his own sovereign prince. There was shortly attached to the office the income from a Flemish canonry. Erasmus traveled back and forth between Basel and various cities of the Low Countries, waiting upon his prince and the great functionaries of the Burgundian court, continuing to work at the revision of the New Testament, which he had already begun, as well as a host of other literary projects—and showering letters in every direction.

There were some unsettling reverses. His councillor's stipend was quickly in arrears. A prebend that Cardinal Wolsey had offered him in the part of Flanders claimed by Henry VIII was conferred upon someone else, and he was left only with the chancellor's promises of another living. But despite occasional grumbling he was reasonably well off, more so surely than he had ever been before. His English pensions were again being paid with some regularity, and the sale of his books now added substantially to his income. Moreover, there was credit if not cash from his court appointment, and there were the gifts of rich friends and powerful patrons. In October, 1516, Erasmus dryly commented to his friend Peter Gillis of Antwerp that the Archduke Charles, now "The Catholic King" of Spain, had offered him a bishopric in Sicily; but he declined the offer, preferring the freedom of his studies.

Shortly his personal situation was to be greatly eased as the favor of Pope Leo was extended to a further and still more comprehensive dispensation from the disability of his illegitimate birth. He had been engaged in arranging this business for some time and had once again enlisted Andrea Ammonio, his Italian friend in England who had been so helpful in the earlier dispensation from Julius II. It was in connection with these arrangements, incidentally, that Erasmus framed the curious autobiographical account contained in his "Letter to Grunnius." The whole affair caused him considerable anxiety, and the exchanges with Ammonio are filled with secretive references to it. But it was accomplished in the spring of 1517, and Erasmus made another hurried trip to England, where Ammonio had received the documents from Rome on his friend's behalf and the authority to dispense him from the pope's own hand.

Erasmus had every reason to be relieved and pleased not only for the improvement of his personal fortunes but for his confidence that, in the larger world, a new age of gold was at hand. In several letters of about this time he expressed himself in exactly that term. In his letter to Pope Leo X declaring his wish to dedicate the St. Jerome edition to him, the following lines occur: "At the very moment of Leo's accession the world suddenly became aware that our worse than iron age had been changed into an Age of Gold."[1] This, like the rest of the lengthy letter, was partly flattery. But Erasmus did view Leo at this point as both a great patron of literature and a great and pacific statesman. He was to be wrong on both counts. For he overestimated Leo's dedication to peace as much as he had misunderstood and hated Julius II's dedication to war. And he assigned much too decisive a role to Rome—whoever sat on the papal throne—in the affairs of the world. But if he was wrong he was at least sincere.

He had similar hopes for the young monarchs just then beginning their reigns in the great European states—Henry VIII of England (1509), Francis I of France (1515), and his own Prince Charles. In the winter of 1517, Erasmus wrote to Wolfgang Capito, a Hebrew scholar who had worked with him in Basel, "I almost wish to be young again, and for the reason that I expect the coming of a golden age: we clearly see how rulers, as if changed by inspiration, devote all their energies to the pursuit of peace."[2]

He saw these rulers not only promoting peace but learning, "gifted men all over the world awaking to the sound of the signal and rising up and joining forces to revive the best learning." Not the least part of this triumph of "the best learning" that Erasmus saw at hand was his own work and the reception it was enjoying from those "gifted men" everywhere. It is true, he continued, that there remain "a few fellows so stupid that they are hooted at even by those of the common rabble who have a little intelligence," who oppose his scholarship, who argue that he threatens the Holy Gospel with his corrections of the text and undermines the authority of the church by his criticism.[3]

I   *The Controversies over the New Testament*

Even as Erasmus wrote these brave and hopeful words to Capito, he knew that his opponents were neither so few nor so contemptible as he claimed. He had tried to anticipate their opposition in the apparatus and the methodological prefaces he had prepared for his New Testament, and he had tried to protect himself by securing the blessing of the pope for the St. Jerome and the New Testament. But his opponents persisted, and the age of gold he had looked forward to so hopefully was tarnished by the acrimony of the controversies that lay just ahead.

The opening volley of these disputes is of some interest. It was the exchange with the Louvain theologian Martin van Dorp, that we have already noted in connection with Dorp's criticism of the *Praise of Folly*. Dorp had written to Erasmus in September of 1514,[4] but Erasmus did not see the letter until a friend in Antwerp showed him a copy of it on his return from the flying trip to England in the spring of 1515. He chose to answer it promptly and at such length as to make it one of the most comprehensive of his many defences of his work and principles. He chose to deal with Dorp's letter in this fashion for a number of reasons. In the first place Dorp had written as a sincerely concerned friend and Erasmus could thus reply in kind. But, at the same time and under the guise of friendly protestation, he could lay out the arguments he wanted to make against those less friendly—in this case his critics in the theological faculty of Louvain—whom he suspected of having made his naive friend the dupe of their own objections, "act[ing] out this playlet behind another's mask."[5] Whether there actually was such a cabal is immaterial. It was the opportunity Erasmus needed for a full-dress rebuttal and he was ready. His work in Basel was hurrying to its conclusion, and scarcely a week earlier he had written his letter to Leo X. Dorp had asked the "right" questions and raised the "right" objections.

He had begun with his objections to the *Praise of Folly*, and we have already dealt with Erasmus's response. Erasmus turns then to Dorp's "wholehearted approval" of his work on St. Jerome. But he will not be placated by approval, for "those whom the *Folly* seriously offends will not approve of this edition of Jerome either" (82). He has already encountered opposition from theologians to any use of Greek or Hebrew in the edition.

Dorp has reserved his most serious objection for Erasmus's proposed Greek New Testament, and Erasmus goes to the heart of his objection:

You do not want me to change anything except where there might be, perhaps, a little clearer meaning in the Greek. You deny that there are faults in the edition we commonly use, and you think that we are forbidden to alter in any way something approved by the agreement of so many ages and so many synods. (84)

But Erasmus points out that Jerome, Augustine, and Ambrose had readings different from the ones we have. What will you do, he continues, when an ancient Greek reading turns out to be approved by St. Jerome, when it is confirmed by ancient Latin codices, and when the meaning fits the context better—yet is different from the Vulgate. "Are you going to disregard all these facts and still follow your own codex, which might have been corrupted by a copyist?" (84). The plain fact is that the Greek was often poorly translated and that the true text has been corrupted by ignorant scribes.

Erasmus makes a special point of Dorp's objection to the use of Greek texts because it was one of the standard objections voiced by the critics of the new learning, i.e., that "we should not rely on the writings of those who fell away from the Roman Church" (85). Erasmus responds:

I can hardly bring myself to believe that you are really sincere in writing this. What are you saying? Shall we not read the writings of people who fell away from the Christian faith? Why, then, do they give such authority to Aristotle, a pagan who never had anything to do with the faith? The whole Jewish race severed itself from Christ; will the Psalms and the Prophets have no importance in our eyes, since they were written in Hebrew? Enumerate all the points on which the Greeks disagree with orthodox Latins: you will find nothing which has come from the words of the New Testament or which is relevant here. (85)

Further, was the Vulgate text ever so approved, he asks, that we are not even allowed to correct its errors? And what of the fact that different copies of this approved text differ one from another?

Erasmus ended his letter on the same friendly note that Dorp "dearest of men" had struck. And indeed their friendship did survive. But other critics, in less friendly fashion, continued to press essentially the points that Dorp had raised. Some argued against anyone's tampering with established tradition and the received texts of religion which, in Dorp's phrase, "contain nothing false or erroneous" and in which the "truth and integrity" of Scripture are inherent. But many critics had special objections to Erasmus's tampering. At best he was a grammarian meddling in theology where he had no business, at worst a Lucianic scoffer whose irresponsible criticisms held up the church and the traditions of centuries to the ridicule of the vulgar. Their case was strengthened by the continuing controversy over the *Praise of Folly*, the deepening suspicion that Erasmus had written the *Julius exclusus*, and even the charge that he was the author of the scurrilous *Letters of Obscure Men*. Their suspicions were further confirmed when the New Testament text and even the Jerome actually appeared. For, in his notes, Erasmus went beyond textual commentary to apply the text—often stretching the point to do so—to the familiar targets of his criticism, the corruption of the clergy, the ignorance of theologians, clerical vestments, empty ceremonies, vows, penance, relics, and, of course, monasticism.

There were, however, other critics not so easily dismissed as those "who did not read my work and would not have understood it if they had"[6]—men who did read and understand his work and who found fault with its substance. And Erasmus, more than anyone, knew there was fault to find. We have already noted his concern over the many errors in the first edition of the New Testament and that he had started to work immediately on a revised edition.

The great French Hellenist Guillaume Budé, while guardedly approving the work, complained that Erasmus dwelt too much on subtleties in his annotations and only picked at a few philosophical points. The French biblical scholar Jacques LeFevre objected to Erasmus's rendering of Hebrews 2:7 in which it is said of Christ, "Thou madest him a little lower than the angels." His objection was on theological rather than linguistic grounds in that such a reading demeaned the stature of Christ. But Erasmus insisted upon the reading. This threatening controversy was at least partially composed by the intercession of mutual friends. Erasmus was involved in a particularly nasty quarrel with the English theologian Edward Lee over his omission of one of the "trinitarian proofs," I John 5:7.

His translation of the New Testament was even more troublesome. His rendering of Matthew 4:17, "Repent: for the kingdom of heaven is at hand," as "be repentant" rather than the Vulgate's "do penance" seemed to threaten the sacrament of penance.

The controversies over his translation of the New Testament worsened when, in the second (1519) edition, the text varied even more radically from the Vulgate. In the opening line of the Gospel of St. John, for example, the famous phrase, "In the beginning was the word," the Vulgate had used the Latin *verbum* for the Greek *logos*. Erasmus translated it with the Latin word *sermo*. He argued that it was a better translation in that it carried the meaning of "discourse" rather than simply "word." But, of course, this term in this context was loaded with implications stretching back to the ancient tradition of logos Christology. And Erasmus was accused of dangerous theological novelty and of casting doubt upon the very incarnation of Christ as "the word."

Even as the successive editions of the Greek New Testament and Erasmus's translation appeared, his popular paraphrases were also being published through the 1520s. Their popularity made them particularly dangerous in the view of Erasmus's critics, for thereby his theological liberalism was the more effectively spread. His enemies compiled lists of his "errors." The Spanish theologian Diego Lopez de Zuñiga (Stunica), one of the polymaths Cardinal Ximenes had employed on the Complutensian Bible, collected 165 of them in a book directed against the "Blasphemies and Errors" of Erasmus. So savage was it that the cardinal forbade its publication, and it appeared only after his death in 1517. From Germany the Dominican theologian of Ingolstadt, Johann Meier von Eck, Luther's famous opponent, attacked Erasmus for what he regarded as demeaning the apostles by even intimating that their knowledge was less than perfect or their Greek less than classical. The theological faculty of the University of Paris, led by Noel Bedier and the Carthusian Jacques

Cousturier, condemned all new translations of the Bible including not only Erasmus's but their countryman LeFevre's. The Louvain theological faculty took similar measures.

The increasingly hysterical tone of Erasmus's critics is to be explained to a large extent not so much by the popularity of Erasmus's writings or even their contents as by the fact that, through the same decade of the 1520s, the Lutheran question was becoming a concern across Europe, from Luther's defiance of Pope Leo's bull *Exsurge Domine* in 1520, through the dramatic confrontation with the young Emperor Charles V at the Diet of Worms in 1521, to the development in the mid-1520s of a well-defined Lutheran party in Germany and an equally well defined Lutheran doctrine that had begun to leak over into the main intellectual-theological stream of European thought. Many, if not most, of Erasmus's more liberal preachments were embraced by the Lutherans and by other radical individuals and sects already beginning to form. It appeared to religious conservatives and to many concerned moderates that Erasmus and his fellow spirits had done more than a little to bring up the storm. And it became distressingly clear to Erasmus that he must take a definitive stand on the problem of Luther.

II   *The Lutheran Storm*

Erasmus's first contact with Luther came in a most casual and indirect way. Georg Spalatin, the Chaplain of Frederick the Wise of Saxony, had written to Erasmus in the winter of 1516—one of those scores of unsolicited letters he had begun to receive from rulers, courtiers, councillors, and men of learning all over Europe, many of whom, like Spalatin, he did not know at all. After introducing himself as a "friend of a friend" and as a pupil of one of Erasmus's old schoolmates from Deventer, and expatiating upon how dear Erasmus was to his master the elector and how admired his books were, he posed a question about a theological point in Erasmus's commentary on the Epistle to the Romans. The point had been raised, he said, by "a certain Augustinian." The unknown Augustinian was Spalatin's friend Martin Luther. Erasmus's reply—whatever it was—apparently never reached Spalatin.

Erasmus did, however, shortly become very much aware of Luther, as did most of the intellectual community of Europe, after the "great indulgence scandal" of 1517 and the circulation of the famous Ninety-five Theses. Erasmus saw them and sent a copy to More and

Colet in England. And he somewhat cautiously approved of them even as he more vigorously opposed the counterclaims already being made in reply to Luther—particularly as these took the occasion to range far beyond the question of indulgences to the most extravagant arguments for papal supremacy. Erasmus was always wary of such arguments and had long since attacked indulgences as sharply as Luther.

But Erasmus was also concerned that the Dominicans especially were becoming heatedly involved in the controversy with Luther. The Dominican Silvestro Prierias, the Master of the Papal Palace, had already published what Erasmus characterized as "an incredibly stupid response,"[7] and he had heard that Eck was beginning his attack on Luther.

In two important and widely circulated letters of 1519—to the Elector Frederick the Wise of Saxony, Luther's prince and protector, and to the Archbishop-Elector Albrecht of Mainz, whose indulgence sale had precipitated the Lutheran crisis—Erasmus carefully developed the precise and narrow base on which he chose to stand regarding Luther. The recipients of these letters were equally carefully chosen, for they represented the polar extremes of political authority on the Lutheran question.

He addressed the Elector Frederick with decorous familiarity—he had dedicated an edition of Suetonius to him two years before—but with the knowledge that the prince was Luther's protector. The letter purposes to encourage that protection in light of the shabby treatment Luther had received in his hearing before the Cardinal-Legate Cajetan at the Augsburg Diet of the preceding year and in light of what Erasmus had heard of Luther's virtue and the purity of his life. He may, he continues, be in error—Erasmus claims no familiarity with his writings though he had probably read them more extensively and more carefully than he was willing to admit—and ventures no judgment on their substance. But Luther has not been instructed about his errors, nor corrected, simply summoned and told to submit. This is a tyranny that a proper Christian prince must oppose. And surely, says Erasmus, Pope Leo wants no such victory.

The letter to Archbishop Albrecht is longer and more detailed. Erasmus had also dedicated a work to him, the preface to the New Testament separately published with the second edition and entitled *Ratio verae Theologiae*. His letter took as its excuse the acknowledgment of the archbishop's gift of a gold cup. After a graceful opening Erasmus gets quickly to the heart of the matter. He states flatly that he has nothing whatever to do with "the case of Luther."[8] From the beginning he has feared that dissension would result from the matter. And although Luther has written him—which in the interval he had done and Erasmus replied—he had advised him against sedition, against criticism of the pope and too arrogantly pressing his cause. But, he continues to the Archbishop, "certain simpletons have interpreted this to mean that I favor Luther" (137). They have even charged that "Luther's books were for the most part mine and that they were written at Louvain" (139). None of this is true. "I am neither Luther's accuser nor his defender, nor am I answerable for him" (137). Erasmus's position is solely that Luther is a good and honest man who deserves to be supported rather than crushed by a "faction of rogues." He wants him corrected rather than destroyed.

As to Luther's so-called doctrines, he really did no more than propose the question of indulgences for academic debate, precisely in the traditional manner of theologians and, in that same tradition, has appealed to the judgment of universities and the Holy See. All this is in sharp contrast to his opponents who "preached indulgences in such a way that even the ignorant could not bear it" and to the detriment of the true spirit of Christ (140). (We may hope the archbishop had the grace to wince a little at this passage!) Luther indeed might have made some "rather extravagant assertions" about indulgences and expressed some reservations about papal supremacy, but his Dominican opponents have been much too extravagant on the other side. Luther has some scruples about the nature of confession, which doctrine has long been abused by the mendicants and interpreted to their own advantage. If Luther is guilty of anything, it is of being "more imprudent than impious" (144).

Erasmus continues that he himself has no quarrel with the notion that the pope is preeminent among bishops and certainly no argument with the present pope. But, he says, "they deserve very ill of him who in their flattery attribute powers to him which he himself does not acknowledge and which are not to the advantage of the Christian flock" (141–42). He sees the real object of their attack as good learning and not least his own role in its revival. They have tried to link him and good learning earlier to the Reuchlin affair and now to Luther. It is for this reason that they cry "this is heresy, this is heresy!" (144). Anything they dislike or misunderstand or suspect is heresy. It is not heresy, he adds; but their persistent clamor is a dangerous tendency that lays all good men open to irresponsible charges and threatens the very church they profess to defend.

These two letters may be said to embody Erasmus's position on Luther as of the autumn of 1519: that is, Luther is a virtuous man and an honorable disputant, taking a legitimate if somewhat too vehement stand in his own cause; he must be heard and, if in error, corrected rather than destroyed; and finally, Erasmus's own program of Christian Humanism must not be confused with support for Luther—they have common enemies, not a common cause.

Even a year later he could still praise Luther, still counsel the Elector Frederick to continue to protect him; and he still had the gravest suspicion of those leading the pack "howling against Luther." But events were rapidly moving beyond the point where Erasmus had resolved to take his own stand. Luther's enemies had finally secured the bull they sought against him from Leo X, dated June 15, 1520. Erasmus disapproved of it as too severe and was convinced that the pope's "good nature" was being exploited. But the bull was a reality. When it was published in Wittenberg in December Luther defied it. In the meantime he had issued a series of tracts more extreme than anything he had uttered thus far, attacking the authority of the pope, the office of the priesthood, and the validity of the sacraments.

In the spring of 1521 Luther was summoned to appear before the emperor at the Diet of Worms. He came, and he defied the emperor as he had defied the pope—Erasmus's own Prince Charles, not only in Erasmus's eyes "by far the noblest and most gentle prince of the faith"[9] but the duly constituted political authority to whom Luther was subject. Erasmus still dreaded the consequences of a victory over Luther by the conservative extremists. But Luther's own actions, the truculence of his language, the intransigence of his theological dogmas, and his clear drift toward a separate and revolutionary religious sect made a reasonable defense of him clearly impossible. Erasmus could no longer defend him.

This, of course, brought down upon Erasmus the wrath of Luther's own extreme partisans, especially Ulrich von Hutten, the German knight and talented humanist writer who had earlier been on very good terms with Erasmus. Hutten had not only become a defender of Luther, but he was advocating open war against the church and now began to accuse Erasmus of deserting the cause he had earlier defended.

On the other side Erasmus continued to be abused by a variety of the same charge—that he "had laid the egg that Luther hatched!" Erasmus himself reported this famous phrase some years later and continued somewhat ruefully, "I laid a chicken egg but Luther hatched a very different kind of bird." He attributed the comment to the Franciscans of Cologne, but it was picked up and repeated everywhere.[10] Cardinal Jerome Aleander, the Papal Legate at the Diet of Worms, and one of Luther's most implacable enemies, expressed essentially the same sentiment. He was also a former friend of Erasmus who had fallen out with him. Writing to Cardinal dei Medici (the cousin of Leo X who would become Pope Clement VII) from Worms in the course of the diet, Aleander complained angrily that Erasmus's New Testament with its notes and commentaries had prepared the way for Luther, that it "brought forth opinions on confession, on indulgence, on excommunication, on divorce, on the power of the pope and on other questions, which Luther had only to take over—save that Erasmus's poison is much more dangerous than Luther's."[11]

There were charges from some Lutheran extremists that Erasmus was the author of Henry VIII's *Defense of the Seven Sacraments*, the book the king had written against Luther which appeared in the summer of 1521. And, at the same time, the extreme Romanists charged that Erasmus was the author of Luther's *On the Babylonian Captivity of the Church* as well as other Lutheran writings. Erasmus's efforts to prevent the public burning of Luther's books simply intensified the suspicions against him even though, at the same time, he was trying to dissuade Froben from printing more of Luther's writings. There was pressure brought upon the University of Louvain to have Erasmus's own books proscribed or searched for "errors." A preacher in Louvain, seeing Erasmus in his congregation, departed from his text "on charity" to attack him "right to my face" as "a strong supporter of Luther." This was the same man, Nicholas Baechem, who, the day before, had capped the ceremony of Aleander's public burning of Luther's books by stepping forward from the crowd and urinating on the embers of the fire. Erasmus was forced to hail him before the rector of the university.[12] Another preacher cried from his pulpit, "Oh that I might sink my teeth in Luther's throat! I would not hesitate even with bloody mouth to go straight to receive the body of Christ."[13]

By the fall of 1521 the third edition of Erasmus's Greek New Testament was ready for the press in Basel. This gave him the welcome pretext to leave the poisonous atmosphere of Louvain. By easy stages he made his way once more to Basel, returning to Froben's peaceful household and the company of his old scholar friends. But Erasmus could no more escape the tumult in Basel than in Louvain, or any place else. The Lutheran question was an issue everywhere. When Ulrich von Hutten—his grandiose scheme for a German war against the church having failed utterly—came to Basel, Erasmus refused to see him, and their simmering quarrel erupted into a violent outburst. In his *Expostulatio* (July, 1523) Hutten charged that Erasmus had "once joined with us to demote the pope," to inveigh "against the cesspool of Roman crimes"; that he had once "detested bulls of indulgence" and "execrated the canon law and the decretals." But "you now turn completely around and join the enemy." He charged him with currying favor with the inquisitor of Cologne (who, by the way, had just presided over a burning of Erasmus's books!) and with the Dominicans (who still thundered against him in every forum they could find). He charged him with defection from the cause of Luther and with selling out the cause of the Gospel, which Hutten clearly saw as one and the same.[14]

Erasmus could not allow such charges to stand. He responded to them in a tract entitled *A Sponge to Wipe Away the Aspersions of Hutten* (September, 1523). It was as testy as Hutten's piece but perhaps a more accurate representation of Erasmus's position in the matter of Luther. But few were as interested as Erasmus in the integrity of Erasmus's position. The Lutheran movement was becoming a revolution, threatening to overturn the civil as well as the ecclesiastical order. Wittenberg was in turmoil and Lutheran doctrines were spreading all over Germany, across the lower Rhine into the Netherlands, the French Rhine provinces, to such cities as Strassburg, and into Switzerland. Erasmus wrote, "I would not dare mention in writing all the places where there is sympathy for Luther and hatred for the name of the Pope, nor would I dare to describe how deeply implanted such feelings are in the hearts of the people."[15] There were already rumblings of wholesale violence that would break out into the great peasant revolt of southern Germany within little more than a year. The demands that Erasmus speak out decisively became more insistent than ever.

Leo X had died in 1521 to be succeeded by another old friend of Erasmus, the Dutch cleric Adrian of Utrecht, as Pope Adrian VI.

They had known each other at Louvain and though Adrian was a somewhat old-fashioned theologian and rather more a statesman than a scholar—he had been the tutor to Charles V, later one of his most trusted advisors, and Charles's influence had weighed heavily in his election to the papacy—he was as much an admirer of Erasmus as he was an enemy of Luther. In the winter of 1522, in an official letter dictated by the pope himself, Adrian invited Erasmus to come to Rome and promised him honors and rewards. Erasmus was relieved, for he knew that Adrian, like his predecessor, was under considerable pressure from the conservative "Romanists" to shun if not condemn him outright. But Adrian also implored Erasmus to take a decisive stand against Luther. He put his request, moreover, in terms Erasmus found hard to refuse. He argued that, as the leading spokesman for the learned community, it was Erasmus's obligation to "reclaim" Luther and his followers from their errors rather than to allow them to be crushed by legal processes and force which Adrian was reluctant to use.[16]

Despite the appeal of the pope's argument, Erasmus politely, elegantly, and firmly refused. It is clear that he hoped to escape the demand that he become a participant in the conflict and to make use of the celebrity to which the pope had referred to stand above the conflict and be its arbitrator. This tactic was, of course, implicit in his earlier position, namely, to encourage Luther in his legitimate complaints against abuses and to condemn those who would have silenced him by force. Now he saw his role as arbitrator as the sole hope of avoiding the bloodshed and open war that seemed so threatening and as the only way to preserve the program of Erasmian Christian Humanism as an authentic alternative to the violent dogmatism of the two extreme factions.

In most of his writings of this time—for example, in the flood of letters that were now often being seized and published before their recipients even got them and in prefaces to such works as his edition of St. Hilary (1523)—Erasmus stresses his hope for arbitration in one way or another. He made his case movingly in a work entitled *On the Immense Mercy of God*. But neither it nor his other pleas brought the concord for which he was appealing.

In some part its failure may be laid to the fact that, in the same work, Erasmus was just as clearly asserting the cause of his own program of Christian Humanism. For what was his call for man's charity to man as the counterpart to God's mercy toward all men except the Erasmian Philosophy of Christ? It is even more important to note, moreover, that Erasmus continued to defend his program not only in such general and irenic terms as those employed in *On the Immense Mercy of God* but in specific detail and with intensified feeling in a cloud of other writings arguing for the spiritual essentials of religion, as he had always done, against the confusion of its purely external trappings and for the correction of the church's abuses that lent such harmful credence to the charges of the reformers. In the 1522 edition of the New Testament, in introductions and prefaces and dedications, in dozens of letters of this time he urged the familiar Erasmian views on the dietary requirements of the church, the excess of saints' days and saint and image veneration, and clerical celibacy. As we have already seen, he wrote some of his most substantial reforming colloquies during this same period of the early 1520s.

Erasmus, in short, refused to allow Luther and the other reformers to preempt the criticism of the church as an issue. In spite of the damaging similarity of many of his opinions to those espoused so forcefully by Luther, he refused to admit the simplistic view that to agree on some points, even some basic points, with the reformers put him in their camp. But this simplistic view continued to prevail among his Catholic critics as did the view among Luther's most extreme supporters that, having encouraged Luther to revolt, Erasmus now abandoned him. It had already become obvious by 1524 that Erasmus could neither stand clear of the conflict nor stand above it. The warring factions were simply too intransigent and Erasmus's own position too subtle and too equivocal. He was compromised by both sides.

III   On Free Will

Even as he finished his *On the Immense Mercy of God*, he had already prepared the first draft of the book against Luther so long demanded of him. It was entitled *A Discourse on Free Will* and was to be the most famous of all Erasmus's controversial works. He handed a draft copy to his friend, the scholar Ludwig Bär, in Basel in February, 1524, for his comments and a month later sent another to Henry VIII. In his note to Bär he claims to have spent, or rather "lost," some "five weary days" in writing it.[17] Recall that he made a similar comment about the *Praise of Folly*. But, like the *Praise of Folly*, this discourse was neither so trivial nor impromptu as such a deprecating statement implies. Indeed, the reverse: there is reason to believe that he had been actively considering the project, perhaps even drawing up his arguments, and certainly settling on the choice of topic as long as a year before.

The issue of free will and grace had been thrust into the forefront of the Lutheran controversy with the bill of particulars appended to Pope Leo's bull *Exsurge Domine*. For the bull specifically condemned Luther's view on the subject. He had stated his view in the course of the public disputation at Heidelberg in 1518 and, after the papal condemnation, did so again in his *Assertio*, in which he wrote, "Since the fall of Adam, or after actual sin, free will exists only in name, and when it does what it can it commits sin."[18] This position was, of course, completely consistent with such basic premises of the Lutheran theology as justification by faith and the assertion of man's total depravity. And Luther had already shown himself prepared to follow the iron logic of his premises.

The issue was perfectly suited to the kind of confrontation Erasmus intended to have with Luther now that confrontation could no longer be avoided. He deliberately chose not to deal with such matters as indulgences for, as we have seen, he intended to maintain his own independent critical position. Nor did he choose the issue of the sacraments, although this was the most obvious area of Luther's disagreement with the church. Again on this complex matter Erasmus had no wish to compromise his own independence. He even avoided the issue of Luther's violence and the social disorder that was springing from it. Although this was one of the most distressing of the implications of Lutheranism for him, he still hoped to promote concord which he could hardly do by violently attacking violence. Nor did he wish to put himself in the camp of Luther's most intemperate critics. He chose instead the old patristic issue of free will and predestination. This put him on the familiar ground of his own philological-historical scholarship. It was, at the same time, one of the most crucial of the theoretical assumptions of Luther's emerging doctrines. It was a question on which Luther had taken a clearly defined position with which Erasmus utterly disagreed and which, moreover, was in flat contradiction to the position of the church. Finally, it went to the heart of the most important theological and philosophical differences between Erasmus and Luther—their fundamental disagreement on the very nature of man, of man's relationship to God, and of God's justice.

In the spring of 1524 Luther wrote Erasmus what he hoped would be a conciliatory letter. He sought no conflict with Erasmus, he wrote. It is enough that Erasmus has given us "God's wonderful and glorious gift" of his biblical studies. But, he continued, "We realize that you have not yet been given by the Lord such courage, or rather such a disposition, that you, together with us, could openly and confidently fight these monsters around us." "Only do not give comfort to my enemies and join their ranks against us. Above all, do not publish booklets against me, and I shall publish nothing against you."[19] Erasmus was offended by Luther's patronizing, even contemptuous, tone, by his charge of cowardice, and perhaps most of all by Luther's implicit denial of the middle position Erasmus had been trying so desperately to maintain. By the end of the summer he had resolved to publish his "booklet," gave it to Froben, and it appeared in print September 1, 1524.

As we have seen, Erasmus intended to restrict the subject to the single question of man's ability or lack of ability "to apply to or turn away from that which leads unto eternal salvation."[20] And he stresses this intention in the preface to the work. He seeks no gladiatorial combat with Luther and no full-scale refutation of his doctrines; but rather a "calm and scholarly" disputation "only against one of Luther's teachings" (5).

Against that one teaching he lays out his opposing view. Man cannot be immobilized by the burden of original sin; we must be able to improve, to be "on the road to piety," and to "forget what lies behind us" (8). Surely we sin in the process, but we have "the remedy of penance" and resort to "the mercy of the Lord, without which neither the human will nor its striving is effective" (8–9).

In contrast, he continues, Luther, following Wyclif, has asserted "that everything we do happens not on account of our free will, but out of sheer necessity." How is it then that we are enjoined by Scripture to love God with all our heart. Who, asks Erasmus, could love "a God who fires a hell with eternal pain, in order to punish there poor mankind for his own evil deeds, as if God enjoyed human distress." But Erasmus is, here as always, as much concerned with behavior as with theology. And he is quick to point out the ethical implications of predestination. Even if it were true, it is a pernicious doctrine to assert to the world, leading weak men "to every impious outrage"—"What wicked fellow would henceforth try to better his conduct?" (12).

Since Luther will recognize no authority but Scripture—his insistence on this point was by now famous—Erasmus agrees to the restriction despite, he reminds his reader, the long speculative tradition that lies behind the question, the authoritative decisions of universities, the decrees of popes and councils, and the fact that Luther seems to claim that he alone in the thirteen-hundred-year history of the church possesses the gift of the Holy Spirit and thus the unique ability to interpret Scripture properly.

Nevertheless, Erasmus will stick to Scripture.

He turns first to the Old Testament proofs supporting free will. The classic text is Ecclesiasticus 15:14–18, "Before man is life and death, good and evil, that which he shall choose shall be given him." Erasmus ties this passage to the pivotal matter of original sin. Adam, he argues, was created not only with uncorrupted reason but uncorrupted will, "quite free, if he wished, to choose also evil" (22). And he did indeed choose evil and passed on his sin to his progeny. But, Erasmus continues, in sharp disagreement with Luther, "our power of judgment . . . has only been obscured by sin, and not extinguished" and our will "has been worsened" "so that it could not improve itself by its own natural means" (22–23).

As he holds thus for a conditioned depravity in man against Luther's assertion of total depravity, so Erasmus sees divine grace not as the single awful decision of election or reprobation for man but as a continuing mechanism of forgiveness, the operation not of God's judgment but of his mercy. "By the grace of God, which forgives sin, the freedom of the will has been restored. . . . Because of the help of divine grace, which always aids his effort, man can persevere in the right state without, however, being freed of his propensity to evil, which stems from the remains of sin once committed" (23). It is this cooperation of God's continuing grace and man's flawed will that permits man to "give alms, pray, practice pious exercises" and generally function as an ethical being. Erasmus rejects utterly the Lutheran view that such works are sin—even when they strive not to be—because of the totality of sin in the creature performing them. "It is incompatible with the infinite love of God for man that a man's striving with all his might for grace should be frustrated." But, nevertheless, man must be free to refuse God's grace, "just as it is our pleasure to open or close our eyes against light" (29).

Erasmus continues with the Old Testament proofs supporting free will. God gave free choice to man in paradise. After the fall, in Genesis 4:6–7, Cain is offered reward for good behavior. In Deuteronomy 30:15–19, man is enjoined to choose to obey or disobey God's commandments. Further evidence is adduced from the prophets in example after example. "The entire Holy Scripture is filled with such exhortations" (34). "It is like looking for water in the ocean" (36).

The New Testament, like the Old, is filled with commandments and exhortations, e.g., "If thou wilt enter into life, keep the commandments" (Matt. 19:17). Take up your cross and follow me; promises of heavenly reward, parables, threats, "Woe to you, Scribes and Pharisees, hypocrites" (Matt. 23:13). Christ's very prayer on the cross, "Father forgive them, for they do not know what they are doing" (Luke 23:34). "How much correcter would it have been to justify them, that they had no free will, and were incapable of acting differently, even if they had wished to do so" (39).

From the Gospels he turns to Paul, "the zealous advocate of grace, who storms the works of [the Jewish] laws" (40), to seek "something which implies the freedom of the will" (40). "Such words as fight, crown, just judge, to give, to fight,—to me—seem difficult to be reconciled with mere necessity, whereby the will does absolutely nothing but endure" (42). In other places Paul calls human sins "the works of the flesh," and not "the works of God" (Gal. 5:19) and insistently implores man to behave, to put off the old man and put on the new, to make himself holy. Erasmus charges that it is plainly absurd "to interpret 'he makes himself holy' to mean 'he is made holy by God, whether he likes it or not'" (44).

Erasmus passes on to the apparent scriptural proof against free will and in support of the position of Luther and Wyclif. There are a handful of passages that seem to make the case. One is Exodus 9:12–16, God's hardening the heart of Pharaoh so that "he would not listen to the laws of God . . . to show you my power and to make my name resound throughout the earth" (46). Another is the matter of God's foreknowledge of Judas's act of betrayal, and another the story of Jacob and Esau, taken to symbolize arbitrary election and reprobation. There are several passages—from Isaiah and Jeremiah to Paul—that make use of the figure "the clay in the potter's hand." These and related passages are treated elaborately and at length, but essentially Erasmus maintains his basic position that man's will cooperates with God's grace and to claim too much for either man's will alone or God's grace alone strains the point.

Erasmus now approaches his conclusion. He has been piling up scriptural proofs establishing the freedom of the will while his opponents have been doing the same on the other side. The reformers have interpreted Scripture so out of a deep concern about the overstress on works and the fact that some "sell them to others according to measurement and weight like selling oil and soap" (79). In contrast, the reformers have turned overwhelmingly to the hope in God's immense mercy "which he gives us plentifully without charge" (80). They have exalted the power of God and emphasized the need for faith as necessary to salvation. "These utterances are also very praiseworthy to me, because they agree with Holy Scripture. They conform to the creed of those who died once and for all to this world" (80). But, ". . . the rational soul in me has many doubts when I hear the following: there is no merit in man; all his works, even the pious ones, are sin; our will can do no more than the clay in the potter's hand, everything we do or want to do is reduced to unconditional necessity" (81).

Luther's absolutism on the question of will raises another difficulty. For the alternative to the denial of free will is to make God the author of evil. "Inasmuch as man can never be the author of good works, he can also never be called the author of evil ones. This opinion seems obviously to attribute cruelty and injustice to God, something religious ears abhor vehemently" (88). To get out of this paradox requires even greater exaggeration and implausibility. Luther must overemphasize original sin; he must minimize God's mercy; he must even diminish God's grace when he argues that "man justified by faith can still do nothing else but sin" (90). He makes God a despicable tyrant to burden man with so many commandments which have no effect but to make his hatred of God the greater and his damnation the more severe.

Luther has replaced the excessive veneration of saints and the specious notion of the treasury of merit with an even greater evil "when he said the saints have no merits whatsoever, and that the works of even the most pious men were sin and would adduce eternal damnation if faith and divine mercy had not come to the rescue" (91). Yet the exaggeration and hardening of Luther's position is paralleled by the same exaggeration and hardening on the other side, with the result that "the whole world is now shaken by the thunder and lightning born of the collision of such exaggerations. If both sides hold fast to their exaggerations, I foresee such a battle as between Achilles and Hector: since both were headstrong, only death could separate them" (92).

The reader must choose whether to believe the opinion of the church fathers and the orthodox tradition or "to accept some paradoxes which are at present disturbing the Christian world" (94), those same paradoxes which, in another place, Erasmus had already declared himself unwilling to die for—the commandments of God, yes, the paradoxes of Luther, no!

Within a few months Erasmus's "booklet" against Luther had gone through seven printings. It was December, 1525, before Luther's response appeared under the title *The Bondage of the Will*. More than a response, it was a savage attack, one of the most shocking examples of polemic in this polemical age. Luther called Erasmus's work "trash . . . refuse . . . ordure" and Erasmus himself "a babbler, a sceptic, and Epicurean hog—stupid, hypocritical, and ignorant of Scripture!"[21] He had delayed in answering Erasmus because Erasmus was not worth answering. His arguments were insignificant, his work contained nothing new and nothing, moreover, that Luther or his associates had not already refuted. "To those who have drunk of the teaching of the Spirit in my books, we have given in abundance and more than enough, and they easily despise your arguments" (98). Nevertheless, Luther continued, "my faithful brethren in Christ press me" to answer Erasmus. And this work is his answer.

Much of Erasmus's argument he contemptuously dismisses as "trivial subtleties" to which he will not respond in detail or in kind. He then proceeds to do so, and at exhaustive length. *The Bondage of the Will* is more than four times as long as Erasmus's *Diatribe*. While Luther's book was as voluminous as it was abusive, he did not in most instances argue his case—he asserted it. On the central point of their disagreement, for example, he wrote, "It is . . . essentially necessary and wholesome for Christians to know that God foreknows nothing contingently, but that He foresees, purposes and does all things according to His immutable, eternal and infallible will. This thunderbolt throws free will flat and utterly dashes it to pieces" (106). On the question of the extent to which man may participate in his own salvation—the point that Erasmus so treasured—Luther is equally assertive: "It is not ourselves, but God only, who works salvation in us" (111). To the extent that Luther addressed Erasmus at all in this long and dogmatic book, his essential point was that Erasmus simply did not understand, he did not "know" as Luther "knew," because he lacked the special illumination of God's grace.

Even as Erasmus failed to persuade Luther he failed to satisfy Luther's most implacable Catholic opponents. He had, it is true, argued persuasively against one of the most fundamental of Luther's theological propositions and, in the process, acknowledged Luther's heresy in endorsing the teachings of Wyclif and Hus on the will, although Erasmus found heresy by association an offensive doctrine. But he had also continued to assert that there were things to be admired in Luther's doctrines as there were things to be abhorred in many facets of the established church. Thus, he had failed to assert papal supremacy and refused to condemn Luther out of hand. He did not defend the full doctrine of penance nor did he condemn justification by faith.

He had hoped to be able to take his position against Luther on a fundamental but specific issue and thus avoid precisely this sort of general condemnation. In short he had hoped to maintain a position on the religious issues of his time independent of both extreme parties. He did not succeed. He further damaged his own hope of independence by responding to Luther's *Bondage of the Will* in a long tract published in two parts, 1526 and 1527, *Hyperaspistes diatribae, A Defence of the Diatribe*. Luther did not even bother to reply. Time and events were leaving Erasmus behind in the increasing isolation of a position he alone seemed to consider worth holding. The wars of the Reformation were at hand.

CHAPTER 5

The Quarrel with No Adversary: Erasmus against War

IN the course of their dispute over free will, Luther had declared that he not only despised Erasmus's dedication to peace, he himself welcomed war, even if the world itself were destroyed and God obliged to create a new one. Such statements and the conviction behind them—expressed not only by Luther but by Catholic militants as well—were rapidly pushing religious controversy toward open warfare in the decade of the 1520s. This rush to violence was more heartbreaking to Erasmus than heresy or theological dissent, more even than the division of the church. For he was a lifelong advocate of peace: this advocacy became one of the leading motifs of his work and thought.

While there are intimations of his concern for peace in his earlier writings, it was only with his visit to Italy, as we have seen, that he came for the first time face to face with the horror of war and the equally horrifying spectacle of the pope's involvement in it. Mrs. Phillips's comment that Julius II "turned Erasmus into a pacifist"[1] has more than a little substance to it. He linked Julius to his hatred for war in the *Praise of Folly* and, more explicitly still, in the *Julius exclusus*. But his most substantial antiwar writings were the adage-essay "Dulce bellum inexpertis" (War is sweet to those who do not know it) of 1515 and the literary oration *Querela Pacis, The Complaint of Peace*, written in 1517.

I "Dulce bellum inexpertis"

The first form of this work, usually simply called the *Bellum*, was a long letter written by Erasmus to Antonius van Bergen, Abbot of St. Bertin, in the Spring of 1514. His purpose was to enlist the considerable influence of the abbot with the emperor and the young Prince Charles in the cause of peace. A truce of sorts had existed among the major European powers since the previous summer. But Erasmus, along with most other knowledgeable observers, was aware how fragile the peace was and that, as he wrote the abbot, "some great disturbances are arising, the issues of which are uncertain."[2] Not the least cause of Erasmus's concern was the rivalry of the great dynastic princes. And that rivalry was intensified in the course of the following few months. The tangle of claims to Italy had not been untangled. Young Henry VIII of England was preparing once more for another "glorious essay" against France. And, within the year in France the aged Louis XII would be succeeded by his young, aggressive, and ambitious cousin, Francis I. It is, in large part, to these princes, their advisors, and those in positions to influence them that the *Bellum* is directed, in the form it took in the 1515 edition of the *Adagia*, not to "the common people and the naturally fickle mob" but to the "princes, whose function should be to restrain with wisdom and reason the rash impulse of the foolish rabble"[3]—while there is still time!

The speculative framework of the essay is established by the rhetorical question, how can man "whom nature made for peace and loving-kindness" get himself involved in such cruel and destructive madness as war? Men's lack of natural armor and weapons, their inherent physical weakness, is symbolic of the fact that they were formed for peace, not war. Rather they were given the power of speech and reason and the need for human society to nurture them. And finally, they were created in the image of the loving God himself.

In contrast Erasmus vividly characterizes the madness and inhuman waste of war—with "the furious shock of battle, and then wholesale butchery, the cruel fate of the killers and the killed, the slaughtered lying in heaps, the fields running with gore, the rivers dyed with human blood." And there are other evils—"the trampled crops, the burnt-out farms, the villages set on fire, the cattle driven away, the girls raped, and the old men carried off captive, and churches sacked, robbery, pillage, violence, and confusion everywhere" (313). There is the more enduring destruction of broken homes and families, hunger and want; and the damage to morals, "contempt of duty, indifference to law, readiness to dare any kind of crime" (314).

Why then do men seek war rather than the peace that is more consonant with their natures? "Worst of all," why do "Christians fight Christians?" "O blindness of the human mind! no one is astonished, no one is horrified" (321). On the contrary, war is blessed from pulpits on both sides and is the object of the most devout prayers.

What is more, such conflict among Christian nations is justified by the arguments of "the just war." Erasmus rejects outright this venerable tradition elaborated by the church itself, reminding his reader that it is specious and falsely based, and arguing rather—as he had enjoined a war of the spirit upon his Christian soldier in the *Enchiridion*—that Christians can justify war only against the real enemies of their religion, "against love of money, against anger, against ambition, against the fear of death" (326). No matter how much legal sanction or justifiable right is claimed for war, he continues, grace must take precedence over every other justification. For the clear Gospel mandate is to repay evil with good; "If someone takes away part of our possessions we must give him the whole" (338) and pray for those who injure us.[4] There is not a scrap of real estate, he points out, to which there is clear and undisputed claim by any given prince and the result can only be that "the whole world is to be entangled with war and slaughter" (341). Even if a "just claim" could be found, consider the cost of asserting it in practical terms: "If we could only take a reckoning and calculate in sober earnest the cost of war and the cost of peace, we should soon understand that peace can be obtained at a cost of ten times less care, effort, hardship, danger, expense and bloodshed than what we spend on war" (326–27). He is essentially pleading that the most unjust peace is to be preferred over the most justifiable war.

He still hopes there is a means to secure peace, even an unjust peace if necessary. "Almost all wars between Christians have arisen from either stupidity or wickedness" (348). But both stupidity and wickedness can be corrected: by reason and learning. Young princes—their wits turned by foolish fables of military glory, their natural impulsiveness and ambition pandered to by flatterers—may still be reformed and educated in virtue.

II   Querela Pacis

The *Bellum* was a popular work: the *Querela Pacis* was more popular still. R. H. Bainton calls it "one of the classics of the literature of peace." It was Erasmus's most comprehensive, most thoughtful, and most popular writing on the subject. There were ten editions of it in its first year and over forty before the end of the century, as well as translations into French, Spanish, English, German, and Dutch. Despite the somewhat greater substance of the *Querela Pacis* and its greater complexity and ornateness, it is in most respects a renewal of the themes dealt with in the *Bellum*. What modifications appear have to do principally with the changes in the political situation in the two years since the *Bellum* was written.

Some, at least, of those "great disturbances" Erasmus had anticipated in 1514 in writing to Antonius van Bergen had indeed come about. In the east the Turkish Empire was beginning to stir once more under the vigorous Selim I. In the west, young Francis I of France had resumed the Italian wars with a brilliant victory at Marignano in 1515. But he then made peace with the Swiss, with the pope in the Concordat of Bologna, and with Erasmus's own Prince Charles at Noyon, giving up his claims to Naples while Charles gave up his to Milan. Charles himself had become king of Spain and was being promoted by Maximilian as his successor to the imperial throne. England and France were still at peace, but the warlike vanities of Henry VIII were by no means satisfied. Indeed, the ambitions and personal rivalries of Henry, Francis, and Charles were linked to the changed political situation in western Europe—especially the threat of Hapsburg hegemony that Charles's varied inheritance raised; and the endless pretexts for war that presented themselves made the continuation of peace among them no more than a hopeful possibility. But it was to this hope that Erasmus appealed. The *Querela Pacis*, like the *Bellum*, was primarily directed to these princes, and specifically to Prince Charles. Erasmus says that it was written shortly after his appointment as councillor to Charles, presumably as part of his duties, and at the request of the Burgundian chancellor Jean LeSauvage. It was dedicated to the great lord Philip of Burgundy, Bishop of Utrecht, ducal and royal councillor, and great-uncle to Prince Charles.

Erasmus's hope for peace was backed by still another feeling, the rising sense of optimism following the publication of his St. Jerome and the Greek New Testament, the sense that "the triumph of good learning" was just around the corner, that with a little help "a new age of gold," an age of learning and piety and good will might be possible—if the fragile peace could be held together. Hence the urgency of his plea for peace in 1517.

The *Querela Pacis*, like the *Praise of Folly*, takes the form of a classical declamation, the Goddess Peace speaking, "complaining" as did Folly that, though she is "the source of all [men's] happiness" and "the protector of the entire race," they have still cast her out, bringing upon themselves "calamity after calamity."[5] Again, like Folly, she asserts her claim to a preeminent position: "Am I not praised by both men and gods as the very source and defender of all good things? What is there of prosperity, of security, or of happiness that cannot be ascribed to me?" (177)—in contrast to war "the destroyer of all things and the very seed of evil" (177). And yet, in spite of this, men expend their effort and intelligence "to exchange me for a heap of ruinous evils" (178).

With the fixing of the rhetorical framework, the similarity between the *Querela Pacis* and the *Praise of Folly* ends. This work is no such *jeu d'esprit* as the *Folly*. It is closer in spirit to the *Enchiridion* and has about it the same earnest, driving, hortatory tone.

The book begins, as does the *Bellum*, with the argument that nature itself is framed not for war but for peace, and man meant for "concord."

Yet it appears that some diabolical fiend has taken over the very heart of man and forced him to reject and destroy these inclinations to tranquillity with an insatiable desire for fighting. (180)

No combination of efforts seems capable of bringing agreement. The logic of nature seems of no consequence among men.

But can we say that Christ is of no consequence among men? Why is it that his most cogent doctrine, that of peace, has no effect among men? If nature is adequate, then why is the more powerful teaching of Christ also ineffective? Why does his urging to mutual benevolence not deter them from the madness of war? (180)

The Goddess Peace then turns to test the validity of her rhetorical question. Is there no place that will welcome her? She finds none. The common people "are as turbulent as the stormy seas" (180). Nor does she find a welcome among the company of scholars, with their parties, quarrels, and factions—"What a disillusion!" (181). She finds no welcome even among the religious; for despite their profession, she finds discord rather than peace.

But what of the courts of princes? They are, unfortunately, "not the home of peace but rather the real source of war" (180). But must this inevitably be the case? "I pray the true Christian prince," he writes, "to behold the image of the chief Prince. If he observes how Christ entered His Kingdom and how He departed the earth, he will understand how He would have him rule. Peace and concord should be the goal" (183). Christ commands the prince "to play the role of minister among his people, not to be superior in just anything but to surpass others in aiding those who need help" (185). And yet, for "small territorial gains" or "a little unpaid money" princes do not hesitate to stir up dissension or shed blood.

One feigns a claim to another's title, another finds a trifling fault in a treaty, or is privately offended by an imagined slight to some-one's wife. But beneath these "vain and superficial" pretexts, there is "the most criminal of all causes of war," "the desire for power," the drive to extend princely authority at the expense of other states (188).

Not the least shameful aspect of war is the involvement of the clergy, from the lowest to the highest: even "the vicars of Christ do not hesitate to instigate the very thing that Christ so detested" (190). In a passage recalling the passion and anger of the *Julius exclusus* he asks, "What has a crosier to do with a sword? What has a Bible to do with a shield? . . . What filth is the tongue of a priest who exhorts war, evil, and murder!" (190).

Once more, as in the *Bellum*, Erasmus suggests the use of ar-bitration, but the notion is not developed further. He has no real confidence in either such an imposed solution as arbitration—even supposing it to be possible—or in the external forms of "leagues or confederacies of men" (193), which, as often as not in his view, contributed to the causes of war. In politics as in religion Erasmus was the advocate of inwardness. "We must look for peace by purging the very source of war, false ambitions and evil desires" (193). His solution lay in the hope of persuading princes to forego those "false ambitions and evil desires" in favor of peace: let them promote what is the common good, let them be as fathers to their families of citizens.

He points to "the self-evident fact that this world of ours is the fatherland of the entire race. If the same nationality binds together those born of the same forebears, if blood relationship fosters amity, if the Church is a great family common to all men, and if the same household can produce concord, is it not foolishness not to accept it everywhere?" (197). "The Fellowship of Christ is the strongest bond of all" (197).

III   *The Antiwar Colloquies and the Despair of Peace*

The last major group of Erasmus's antiwar writings are those that appeared among the colloquies of the 1520s, such as "Military Affairs" (1522) and "The Soldier and the Carthusian" (1523). They all show an increasing savagery of satire that makes them very like the *Julius exclusus* but rather unlike the *Bellum* or the *Querela Pacis*. But these latter two works had sprung, as we have seen, from the hope of peace. Now that hope was gone.

The incipient hostility of Charles V and Francis I had come to open war in 1521, principally in northern Italy. In 1525 Francis had been defeated and captured at the battle of Pavia and carried off prisoner to Madrid, where he finally agreed to a treaty ending the war. No sooner was he released, however, than he repudiated the treaty, leagued himself with the pope against Charles, and entered upon a second round of war. In 1527 the imperial forces in northern Italy mutinied and marched on Rome, subjecting it to the most terrible destruction in all its long history. In the east in 1520 the greatest of the Turkish sultans came to power, Suleiman the Magnificent, and turned his formidable strength fully against the west. The key fortress of Rhodes, defended by the Knights of St. John, fell to the Turkish fleet in 1522. In the previous year the Turkish capture of Belgrade had opened central Europe to attack. In 1526 King Louis II of Hungary was killed and his army annihilated at the battle of the plain of Mohács. Following Mohács both Buda and Pest fell. And in 1529 Vienna was under Turkish siege.

Erasmus's hope that Leo X would lead the world to a new era of peace had been dashed. Then, after the brief reign of Adrian VI, Leo's cousin had become Clement VII and dedicated himself not to a policy of peace but to alliance with the warring secular powers which had laid his city open to the terrible "sacco di Roma" and brought the papacy to a low point in its prestige.

Lutheranism had become a militant political movement. By the end of the decade a powerful party of Lutheran princes stood ready to oppose the emperor in open warfare and splinter groups of Protestants of every persuasion were already appearing, often as ready to die or kill for their convictions as were the Lutherans.

Erasmus's efforts to moderate the religious conflict, like his efforts to perpetuate the peace, had come to nothing. And, as we have seen, he himself was caught between the polarizing forces of religious war, discredited by both extreme Protestants and militant Catholics. Erasmus's hope for peace in the preceding decade gave way to despair, and his despair culminated, more than in any other work, in the colloquy "Charon" (1529). Robert P. Adams calls it the "most sinister of all his writings against war."[6]

It was certainly his most savage and intense and was contained in a single devastating scene, set in hell. The spirit Alastor meets his friend Charon, the infernal boatman. Alastor is glad to run into Charon for he was on his way to see him anyhow, with the news that "there'll soon be such a crowd of shades coming that I fear you can't ferry them all."[7] But Charon is already aware of it and is about to take delivery on a "good, strong trireme," for "my galley's so rotten with age and so patched up that it won't do for this job" (390).

They start to talk about the reasons for the unusual traffic in souls. Charon notes "that the three rulers of the world [Charles V, Francis I, and Henry VIII], in deadly hatred, clash to their mutual destruction," and that the "new epidemic" of Lutheranism gives him "hopes of a splendid slaughter in the near future, too, if the war of tongues and pens comes to actual blows" (391).

This discourse is followed by an ironic passage on Erasmus's own fruitless campaign for peace. Charon says, "But there's danger that some devil will turn up and preach peace all of a sudden." In fact, he says, "I hear there's a certain Polygraphus [writer of many books] up there who's incessantly attacking war with his pen and urging men to peace." But Alastor reassures Charon, "He's sung to deaf ears this long while. He once wrote a 'Complaint of Peace O'erthrown'" and—a kind of ultimate irony directed at this colloquy itself—"now he's written the epitaph of peace dead and buried (391).

As if to underscore the failure of the pacific Polygraphus, Alastor notes, "On the other hand, there are some as helpful to our cause as the furies themselves." These, of course, turn out to be Erasmus's old foes, the mendicant orders, inciting "rulers and populace alike," proclaiming in their evangelical sermons "that war is just, holy, and right" (391–92).

The two speakers return to the subject of Charon's new boat and his concern over the increasing volume of business. Alastor raises the question of the incorporeal nature of souls. How heavy can they be? But Charon explains, "They may be water skippers, but enough water skippers could sink a boat" (392). Furthermore, what about vigorous, well-fed soldiers, caught in the midst of life, and "loaded

not only with debauchery and gluttony but even with bulls, benefices, and many other things" (393). Alastor again protests: surely
his friend exaggerates, for "none of those who die in a just war come
to you, I believe. For these, they say, fly straight to heaven" (393).
Charon does not bother to debate the theological point; he simply
says, "Where they may fly to, I don't know. I *do* know one thing:
that whenever a war's on, so many come to me wounded and cut up
that I'd be surprised if any had been left on earth" (393).

There is, however, one further problem with the ship, one further
delay. "We're short of timber," Charon explains. "Even the groves
in the Elysian fields have been used up . . . for burning shades of
heretics." The discourse of reason in religion has come to the same
violent end as has political debate. And, in the meantime, the souls
of the slaughtered await transport, "over two hundred thousand on
the bank already, besides those swimming in the swamp." "Tell 'em
I'll be there right away," says Charon as his fellow spirit departs
(394).

IV   *From Pacifism to Politics*

The strength of Erasmus's pacifism flowed from moral and religious conviction rather than from a consistent, well-developed
political philosophy; indeed, the lack of such a philosophy is the
most obvious weakness of Erasmus's "program for peace."

In theoretical terms he often expressed a preference for the con-
ciliar arguments on ecclesiastical government, particularly as in the
case of a bad pope. He argued in the *Julius exclusus* that such a pope
could be removed from office. But he remained a reformer rather
than a revolutionary in church polity. On several occasions he expressed the view that secular governments derive their just powers
from the consent of the governed. He even speaks, in the *Querela
Pacis*, of "a general election of the people" (194) and was not un-
sympathetic to such institutions of popular sovereignty as assem-
blies and parliaments. Still he was always ambivalent about "the
people," often compassionate about their suffering under war and
tyranny, equally often contemptuous of them as "a naturally fickle
mob" or a "foolish rabble." Although he was clearly aware of the
power of emerging nationalism—indeed his chief criticism of the
"just war" theory was that no court of last resort existed to decide
the issue of justice among sovereign nation states—he never really

understood national sentiment and tended to treat it lightly as a mere matter of "dissimilarity of names" or to denounce it with angry impatience when it contributed to war.

But such views as these never coalesced into a corpus of theory. Erasmus remained fundamentally a rather conservative monarchical legitimist in his notions about both church and state and held to equally conservative notions on the fixed nature of the social and political order. Among the many things he was, Erasmus was not a political theorist. One has only to compare him with his contemporary Machiavelli or even with his great friend Thomas More. In spite of the fact that he lived through the first great age of modern "macht-politik" and that he strongly sensed its impact upon the purposes of his own life and thought, he was simply not interested enough in politics either to sustain a long and complex inquiry or to develop a coherent general theory. He was unwilling to divert his energies from matters he deemed more pressing.

This had the result, as we have observed, of limiting the effectiveness even of his program for peace. In both the *Bellum* and the *Querela Pacis*, for example, he proposed the international arbitration of disputes among nations. But, though he suggested that there were wise and learned men to do the arbitrating, he had to know also that there was no juridical machinery for such arbitration, and he proposed none. Alternatively he proposed that the pope might serve to settle differences among nations. He probably had in mind the role Leo X had played in bringing peace between France and England in 1514. But Leo's part in that affair was very slight, and in most cases the papacy was too compromised by its own involvement in the tangle of European politics to be seriously considered as an international arbiter. In the *Querela Pacis* Erasmus says "there should be some kind of agreement" that once the borders of a state are fixed they remain inviolate and that no alliance "be allowed" to destroy them (194). He does not tell us how the "agreement" is to be made nor how it is to be kept "inviolate." He is contemptuous of such causes for conflict as "small territorial gains," "a little unpaid money," disputed titles, the tiresome details of treaties and marriage alliances—the very stuff of dynastic politics. But, bad or good, the existing system of European dynastic politics had to be dealt with in any realistic program for peace. Instead of dealing with it, Erasmus alternately scolded the princes and exhorted them to Christlike behavior. In the *Querela Pacis* he observed that it did not really matter "who ruled a kingdom so long as the welfare of the people was seen to" (188). It did matter, of course, and it mattered to the princes who, by Erasmus's own admission, played the major role in the political decisions of his time.

Despite the unrealistic idealism of his approach to princely power, Erasmus did know that the princes mattered, that the most serious disputes among nations arose precisely from "the desire for power" in their rulers. As we have seen, he did address the princes time and again in his writings on peace. His principal point in this regard is expressed in one of the adage-essays of the 1515 *Adagia*, "Aut fatuum aut regem nasci oportere" (Kings and fools are born not made). In it he wrote that hereditary monarchy is "a thing we cannot change." "The next best plan would be to improve matters by careful education." "If we may not choose a suitable person to be our ruler, it is important to try to make that person suitable whom fate has given us."[8]

This theme was sounded often in his antiwar writings but it became the chief burden of a book entitled *Institutio Principis Christiani, The Education of a Christian Prince*. Like the *Querela Pacis* it was written as part of Erasmus's duties as a councillor to Prince Charles and dedicated to him in the spring of 1516, clearly anticipating Charles's accession to the throne of Spain.[9] In spite of Erasmus's assertion later[10] that Charles did not take offense at his plain speaking and manfully bore his spirited counsel, there was little in the book that might have given offense.

More than most of his books this one tends to be a tissue of quotations and conventional wisdom. It is based mainly on Isocrates with a liberal mixture of Xenophon, Plutarch, Cicero, and the usual Christian moralists. The modern editor of the *Institutio* says it is "full of platitudes, repetitions, and miscellanies."[11] Many of its substantive ideas were simply restated from earlier writings—Erasmus's caution about social innovation, his suspicion of treaties and alliances, his disapproval of princely marriage or princely travel outside one's own realm. And this was written for Charles, who would court marriage alliances all over Europe and who would log more miles in travel than any ruler of his time!

A large part of the work seconds Erasmus's writings against war, but mainly it is directed to the theme already stated, namely, that, given an hereditary prince and the conviction that, at its best, monarchy is the most preferable form of government, then it is the duty of wise counsel to instruct the prince. The *Institutio* is thus an instance of the *Speculum Principis* genre. What is important, however, in view of the foregoing argument, is that it is not a handbook of politics; it is rather a handbook of morals. Erasmus himself later included it in the catalog of his writings among a group of works intended for "instruction in reasonable and pious living."[12] It is consistent with his view that politics and political issues must be considered in terms of their ends rather than their means, that is, order, concord, the Christian life. The focus of his thought, whether religious or secular, was always on the inner man. The Philosophy of Christ was to derive from an inner conviction and express itself in individual moral conduct. In the *Institutio* Erasmus asserted "that the teachings of Christ apply to no one more than to the prince" (148) and that it is proper for princes "to take their pattern of government" only from Christ, "the one Master of Christian men" (177). This was sound advice but advice at once so simple and so profound that it could only be ignored.

We have no evidence that Charles ever took the *Institutio* seriously. Erasmus tells us that when he revised it, in 1518, and presented it to Charles's brother Ferdinand, that grateful prince later informed him the book was never out of his hand. This was, at the most optimistic, no more than a graceful compliment. Erasmus was surely more right when he observed in the colloquy "Charon" that he had "sung to deaf ears this long while"—both as to his hope for peace and his hope for a political order in which peace might flourish.

CHAPTER 6

Epilogue and Last Years

W E have treated Erasmus principally as a literary figure, dealing at length with his books of most enduring literary quality and with the handful of ideas that shaped his work and his life: his unflagging devotion to "bonae litterae," that made him "the prince of humanists"; his commitment to what we have called, in his own phrase, the *Philosophia Christi*; his persistent concern with the reform of traditional religion; and his passion for peace. But, like great men of letters in every age, Erasmus had things to say on a wide range of topics often neither strictly literary nor strictly philosophical. Boundaries between topics never seemed to exist for him.

I Catalogus lucubrationum

He was, for example, the most popular and widely read educational writer of his time, and long afterward. As we have already seen, his famous *Colloquies* originated as instructional exercises for the private tutorial pupils he was forced to take during his lean years as a student at the University of Paris in the late 1490s. This was the case also with the *De Copia*; a book on letter writing; and probably others, including the earliest form of the *Adagia*. Erasmus maintained the most cordial relations with several of these Paris pupils, some for many years. As we have also seen, he managed his long-delayed trip to Italy by serving as a sort of supervisor of studies for the sons of the physician Boerio and later as preceptor to Alexander Stuart. He remained very fond both of the young Scots nobleman and the Boerio boys. For nearly all his life Erasmus kept a series of pupil-servants who would take care of his household needs, serve as secretaries, proofreaders, copyists, and generally be literary apprentices to him. He liked to call them by the classical term "famuli" and affectionately referred to them as his "familia" or "nostra academia." Several of them became themselves distinguished men of letters, scholars, teachers; and nearly all of them adored Erasmus.

But despite these instances, Erasmus did not like regular, formal teaching and avoided it whenever possible. There were only two times in his life when he held institutional academic appointments—a loose affiliation with the University of Louvain in 1504 and a Cambridge professorship from 1511 to 1514. Both were assumed under some duress and the years at Cambridge especially were filled with grumbling about his colleagues and his duties. Nevertheless, Erasmus had the greatest respect for the importance of teaching and the role of the teacher. There is a passage in a letter to a discouraged schoolmaster of Schlettstadt, Joannes Witz (Sapidius), that conveys some of Erasmus's sense of the importance of the teacher. "As for your vocation," he writes,

I admit it is laborious, but I utterly deny that it is a tragic, as you call it, or deplorable position. To be a schoolmaster is next to being a king. Do you reckon it a mean employment to imbue the minds of your fellow citizens in their earliest years with the best letters and with the love of Christ, and to return them to their country honest and virtuous men? In the opinion of fools it is a humble task, but in fact it is the noblest of occupations.[1]

Erasmus moved constantly through the fringes of the European academic community—Paris, Oxford, Cambridge, Bologna, Basel, Louvain. In Louvain he was even involved in setting up a new college, the *Collegium Trilinguae*, in which Latin, Greek, and Hebrew would be taught—a scheme he had proposed to his wealthy friend Jerome de Busleiden and which was provided for in Busleiden's will following his death in 1517.

Erasmus's most fruitful association with any educational institution was, however, with the Cathedral School of St. Paul's in London. His great friend John Colet had been appointed dean of the cathedral chapter in 1504. In 1510, as part of his effort to reform the chapter, he used his own sizeable family fortune to reendow the school, and he sought Erasmus's help and advice. Erasmus politely declined to serve as its headmaster but, short of that, he enthusiastically entered upon his friend's venture with him. As he preferred to be the theologian's theologian, he preferred to be the schoolmaster's schoolmaster. He helped shape the ideas Colet wanted put into effect, suggested candidates for the staff, and turned into Latin verse a catechism Colet had written for the school. He revised a Latin syntax which was originally prepared by William Lily, whom he had recommended to Colet as the first headmaster. In addition he wrote several substantial books for use in the school. The *De ratione studii ac legendi interpretandique auctores liber* was a handbook for teachers, a carefully reasoned plan for instruction in Latin and Greek, with a canon of authors to be studied. The *De Copia Verborum ac Rerum Commentarii duo*, which Erasmus had worked on intermittently and then lost when he was in Italy, was revived and completed for St. Paul's. It was a work on rhetorical amplification, that "varying of discourse" so prized by Renaissance rhetoricians.

At the same time he was working again on a treatise on letter writing which, like the *Copia*, he had mentioned as being "in hand" off and on for many years. This work, however, was not finished until 1522 but shortly became the most authoritative book on its subject by the greatest letter writer of his age. By this time, of course, the revised editions of the *Colloquies* were beginning to appear. In 1529 his important systematic tract on educational method was published, the *Declamatio de pueris statim ac liberaliter instituendis*. And there were others, including at least two collections resembling the *Adagia*, the *Parabolae sive Similia* (1514) and the *Apophthegmata* (1531); and even a charming little commentary on a work mistakenly attributed to Ovid, *Nux, The Complaint of the Walnut Tree*, likely intended as a study aid for Thomas More's son John. Others of his writings were used in schools that were not, strictly speaking, intended for that purpose, for example, many of his Greek translations and the collections of his letters. We have already commented upon the wide use of the *Colloquies*. His *De recta Latina Graecique sermonis pronuntiatione Dialogus* was used as a school text but was actually part of the acrimonious linguistic controversy that provoked the *Ciceronianus* in the late 1520s.

Erasmus's educational writings were testimony to his conviction that men really could be reformed by learning and that evil was generally the result of ignorance—"good books make good men!" It was a theme running through nearly all his writing. But it was not his purpose that made his school books appealing. It was their style. They were lively rather than dull, interesting enough to keep the attention even of laggard schoolboys. And they were peppered with his own views on a wide range of subjects. But in the long run their substance, even their stylistic appeal, was probably less important than the broad, generous, and humane spirit that invests them. In his educational works, the best of Erasmus is seen at its best.

Not unexpectedly, Erasmus had almost no interest in science or technology. Medicine was the sole exception and that only because his own illnesses gave him an almost neurotic interest in the subject. Perhaps for that reason he was sympathetic to suffering in others and had definite and sensible ideas about such subjects as diet and personal hygiene. Time and again he fled pell-mell and unheroically at the onset of the plague; but recall that both his parents had died of it and he himself was severely stricken on at least one occasion. And, of course, he had a loathing of syphilis. But even his interest in medicine was more appreciative than clinical. He praised Kopp, Paracelsus, and Linacre, all of whom treated him at one time or another, and, on one occasion, he wrote Linacre asking him to send a particular prescription he could not get filled on the continent. He did edit a work of Galen, *Exhortatio ad bonas arteis, praesertim medicinam, de optimo docendi genera, et qualem oporteat esse medicum* (1526). It was, however, not a scientific text but a plea for physicians to know "bonae litterae." He also edited Pliny's *Historia Naturalis* (1525), and two of the colloquies, "Sympathy" (1531) and "A Problem" (1533), were directed respectively to natural history and Aristotelian physics. But in all of these his interest was in the text and vocabulary, not the substance. His interest in mathematics was purely conventional.

The astronomical speculations of his great contemporary Copernicus were, if not completely unknown to Erasmus, certainly of no great interest to him. To his credit—and in contrast to Luther and most of the other reformers—he had nothing but contempt for the whole flock of pseudosciences like astrology and divination and the cabalistic lore that edged into witchcraft, demonology, magic, and the occult.

He seems to have had almost no interest in the great geographical discoveries of his age. He did praise his friend More's *Utopia*, but the praise went to the man and the message, not necessarily to the ingenious story framework derived from the tales of the New World. Otherwise Erasmus mentions the great discoveries only two or three times and quite casually in all his vast correspondence, and deals with the subject not at all anywhere else.

He had no particular interest in music, unlike Luther, and not even a casual competence in it as many of his friends did. In spite of a doubtful tradition that he studied painting in his youth, he had no very great interest either in the visual arts or architecture. He occasionally mentions some work or monument but almost never describes it. On his trip to Italy he expressed no interest in the artistic traditions of Florence or Venice and made not even one passing reference to the great artistic and building projects going on in Rome. Raphael, Michelangelo, Leonardo, and Titian were all at work at that time in the Italian cities he visited; yet he did not mention them. He did know the great northern artists Metsys, Holbein, and Dürer, all of whom did portraits of him. He was especially fond of Holbein who illustrated a copy of the first Froben edition of the *Praise of Folly*. When Holbein later went to England to do his remarkable series of court portraits he carried a letter of introduction from Erasmus. One of his finest works is his portrait of Erasmus's friend More, as chancellor. Erasmus seldom refers to landscapes and, indeed, except for an occasional depiction of a garden setting for some literary or philosophical conversation, his works are bare of descriptions of nature.

Somewhat curiously, Erasmus had no very strong sense of history and no particular interest in its systematic study. He wrote no work of history himself. He knew the classical historians, of course, and even did some translations and editions of them. He prepared editions of Suetonius (1518), Livy (1530), and translated a small work of Xenophon (1530). He was involved in the edition of a fragment of Josephus, though he may only have done the final editing of the Latin text. Although Plutarch was one of his favorite Greek authors and he translated several of his works, these included none of the famous historical biographies. He mentions some more recent historians, for example, in the famous "slam list" of the *Ciceronianus*. He may have been acquainted with Platina's *History of the Popes*. But there is no indication that he was familiar at all with most of the great humanist historians such as Bruni or Flavio Biondo. The same was true of the historical writers of his own generation. He was in England and closely associated with Thomas More at the time More was at work on his *Richard III*, but Erasmus never referred to the work. He also knew Polydore Vergil and was more than slightly interested in some of his writings, but he expressed no interest in his most important work, the *Historia Anglica*.

Erasmus was content to mine the vast literature of history for *exempla*—the *Adagia*, for instance, is filled with historical references as are his other writings—on an array of subjects. Yet he embraced no theory of history nor did he feel that the study of history in and of itself was an avenue by which truth could be arrived at, at least not the kind of truth he was interested in. Indeed the reverse: he profoundly distrusted the tendency of history to glorify conquerors and military victors, "the greatest rogues," and thus make them objects of imitation.

On the other hand, the notions of temporal perspective and historical distance were essential to his sacred scholarship, with its constant resort to the age of the early church. In instance after instance, in the prefaces and notes to his patristic editions, he demonstrated that the true interpretation of a text depended upon understanding the peculiar historical setting that produced it. Yet he was strangely disinterested in the biographies of the fathers themselves in those same notes and particularly in his prefaces to their works. The one exception was St. Jerome. For this favorite of his among the fathers Erasmus went to unusual pains to search his works for historical references, to flesh out and people Jerome's controversies, and to reconstruct the setting of his life. Yet this was his "only full-fledged biography."[2]

He did write several biographical sketches, the most famous being his sketch of Thomas More in a letter to Hutten in 1519,[3] before their falling out, and a double sketch of Colet and Jean Vitrier in a letter to Justus Jonas in 1521.[4] These sketches, like the more substantial work on Jerome, were often vivid in calling up a facet of personality or recreating a scene. But on the whole Erasmus was much more interested in characterizing his subjects than in describing them, even "his derling" More. This may provide us a clue to Erasmus's general feeling about biography, and about history. While men have biographies and events have histories, character and morality do not. And these latter were the ultimate concerns of Erasmus. Thus his interest in biography was to instruct other men by the delineation of the good character of some men. His interest in history was to instruct his own age in the examples of morality and true doctrine that he found in the age of the early church. That age became for him a kind of age of gold to which he constantly directed the attention of his contemporaries, and he showed comparatively little concern for the events of the intervening centuries between that "best of times" and the "tragicum saeculum," his own "worst century."

II   *The Last Years*

The tumult of that "worst century" finally reached even to the sanctuary of Basel. In the late 1520s the attacks of his enemies and the charges of his critics and the rapidly changing tempo of the whole European scene increased Erasmus's apprehension. The papacy under Clement VII (1523–1534) had no such special ties of sympathy with him as he had enjoyed under either Leo X or Adrian VI. In 1527 Clement authorized the Inquisitor General, the Spanish Cardinal-Archbishop of Seville, Alonzo Manrique, to make formal inquiry into the charges of Lutheran doctrine in Erasmus's writings. He was saved from serious embarrassment only by the personal good will of the inquisitor and his own ties to the emperor. But the strident criticism of his works in Spain continued, especially from a group of monks. Erasmus replied with his *Apologia ad monachos Hispanos* in 1528 and again, with another edition, in 1529. At the same time he was involved in a bitter, name-calling controversy with the Spanish Franciscan Luis Carvajal. Carvajal called Erasmus's writings "trifles" and Erasmus called Carvajal's *Apologia* "feverish" and him "a louse."

The same sort of criticism and the same sort of charges were being made against him in France, where the critics were led by Noel Bedier, a conservative theologian and official of the Sorbonne. Under Bedier's prodding the faculty condemned several of Erasmus's works and portions of others. The Lutherans continued their accusations that Erasmus was "two faced," cowardly, and a false prophet. Luther called him an "amphibian."

But it was not the distant Lutherans who made life increasingly miserable for Erasmus: it was the nearby Sacramentarians. This term has come to be used—Erasmus used it himself[5]—to describe, somewhat loosely, a group of the younger, second-generation reformers, generally those who raised questions about the traditional sacraments and, in particular, tended to a figurative interpretation of the mass. Zwingli may be said to have belonged to this group, and Erasmus had already broken with him. Both Carlstadt and Müntzer, read out of the Lutheran camp, came to Basel where they were as thoroughly repugnant to Erasmus as they had been to Luther. Guillaume Farel, another radical reformer from France and the future associate of Calvin in Geneva, came to Basel where he quarreled with Erasmus. Bucer and Capito in Strassburg he contemptuously called *Pseudevangelici*. Despite Erasmus's disapproval of these radicals, they were uncomfortably close to many of the things he had long advocated—the preference for the inward spirituality of religion as opposed to its outward forms, the disapproval of relics, saints, pilgrimages, indulgences, and monasticism; even their tendency to interpret the sacraments in a spiritual manner was more Erasmian than otherwise. Where they differed from Erasmus was that they sought to carry their programs into practice, violently if necessary. They would change the liturgy, simplify worship, deny the saints, destroy the images, repudiate any ecclesiastical authority but their own and "the word of God"—and force others to subscribe to their reform. It was unimportant to them that in insisting upon their "Erasmian" reforms they violated the even more fundamental Erasmian concerns for love among Christians, brotherhood, and concord.

In Basel, as in other Swiss cities, the Reformation came at the level of community consent, with factions forming to support one confessional view or another before the town council and the citizenry. Erasmus counseled moderation, here as everywhere else, but he did not long prevail against Joannes Oecolampadius, who had been his friend and one of his associates in the work of the New Testament. Oecolampadius was now the pastor of one of the city's churches, an active reformer, and the leader of the sacramentarian faction. Before the winter of 1529 was through, debate and orderly disputation had given way to violence. The university was closed, and there were riots in the city. The great münster of the city as well as other churches were stormed by mobs and their images, windows, and treasures smashed. As a result the town council was intimidated into accepting Oecolampadius's version of the reformed doctrine. The mass was abolished, along with the rest of the old religion, and evangelical services were made compulsory for all citizens. Basel had become a microcosm of the larger world of intolerant factionalism. It was too much for Erasmus.

By early March he was quietly beginning to look for another residence. He was attracted to the Netherlands. Despite his disputes with the Louvain theologians he still had powerful friends at court and was still an imperial councillor. But the emperor was increasingly absent in Spain, and Erasmus had no desire for the long journey nor for that strange country which seemed so hostile to his ideas—though even there he had his champions. Rome attracted him too, for he was still unaware of the pope's disaffection. England had been at one time a second home to him, and it was still attractive, but the political climate there was becoming overcast with the king's "great matter," and Erasmus had already written in favor of Henry's embattled queen. There was still France and "our Germany." Indeed, it made comparatively little difference to Erasmus where he went. Two years earlier he had written, "I have never really preferred one place over another. The whole world is my fatherland. I am so fond of the best in letters that I am drawn to any who practice them and count these my kinsmen."[6]

There was no dearth of invitations, some from as far away as Poland. For despite controversy and suspicion Erasmus was still the most famous literary figure in Europe. Anton Fugger twice invited him to come to Augsburg, the second time offering to provide a house for him. The emperor's brother King Ferdinand invited him to Vienna. It was finally Ferdinand's hospitality he accepted, not to come to distant Vienna but to nearby Freiburg in Breisgau. The town was within Ferdinand's lands, was reasonably quiet, and, doubtless at Erasmus's prompting, the king commended him to the town council and made one of his own residences available to Erasmus. Wherever he might otherwise have chosen to go, Erasmus was simply too frail for a long journey. Even his removal to Freiburg was delayed by illness. But on April 13, 1529, his possessions having been sent on ahead, he took his leave of Basel from the bridgehead landing. He was accompanied part of the way by Boniface Amerbach, and, although there was some momentary question about his being permitted to leave, Oecolampadius did see him off civilly enough for all their differences. And a considerable crowd watched silently as their most distinguished resident departed, a refugee from their own religious tumult.

Life in Freiburg was not unpleasant despite complaints about high prices and some wrangling over the rental terms of his house. He was honored by the university and received a nominal appointment to its faculty. He took to the climate of Freiburg, and, to his own surprise, his health improved slightly. He was even able to visit Besançon, and his spirits were also improved by sampling again its "good Burgundian wine." He finally resolved to end the tiresome dispute about his living quarters and bought a house. He complained of the cost to his friend and banker Erasmus Schets of Antwerp and to others; and he complained about the nuisance of moving and decorating and dealing with workmen. He would rather endure three years of his accustomed work than a month of such confusion.

But his accustomed work went on with scarcely an interruption for the moving or for the bouts of illness that now came with increasing frequency and racked "my poor little body." These were, in fact, extraordinarily productive years, and his working conditions had never been better. Students from the university served as *famuli*. His works included further editions and translations of the church fathers. He was beginning to gather the notes for another edition of the New Testament and a definitive edition of Origen. There were such pagan classics as a second, expanded edition of Seneca (1529), Xenophon's *Hieron* and a revised Suetonius (1530), Livy and Aristotle (1531), Terence (1533), and a new edition of his favorite pieces from Plutarch. There was a new edition of the *Adagia*, dedicated to Mountjoy's son, the preparation of the *Apophthegmata* (1531), and a new edition of the *De Copia* (1534). There was a treatise on the method of preaching that he had been promising for years and intended for his old benefactor and friend Bishop Fisher; a humble and moving little tract on the preparation for death; a commentary on the Twenty-third Psalm done at the request of Sir Thomas Boleyn; and successive collections of his letters.

But the concord of the world remained his obsession and his despair. Erasmus, as most like-minded men, had looked forward hopefully to the great meeting of the Imperial Diet scheduled for Augsburg in the summer of 1530 at which the emperor Charles himself would preside and at which he had announced he would make a definitive decision on the question of his relations with the Protestants. Erasmus was pointedly omitted from the list of dignitaries: his health would not have permitted him to go in any case. But invitations went to the major reformed sects, not only the Lutherans but the Sacramentarians, the Swiss and Strassburg reformers. Erasmus refrained, out of deference, from writing to the emperor, whom he still praised to others, but he did write to other councillors who would be present, to the papal representatives, and even to Phillip Melanchthon, who was to make the Lutheran case. These letters are full of Erasmus's observations on the political situation of the moment, including the Turkish threat in eastern Europe, and his pleas for moderation, for further concessions to be made if necessary to the sectaries, but for peace at virtually any price.

But Charles was not disposed to make further concessions. The second round of his wars with Francis I had ended to his advantage with the Peace of Cambrai in the previous year, and he now intended to turn his full strength against the hated Protestants. There were indeed precious few at the diet who wanted peace, no matter what the cost. The principal document that was laid between the factions was the famous Augsburg Confession, drawn up by Luther, who was not present, and revised by Melanchthon, who was, and who was also willing himself to make concessions for the sake of peace. But what is more important, the Confession was the bottom line of concession on the part of the Lutheran princes. And Charles rejected it, summarily. Charles further refused even to look at the *Apologia* prepared by Melanchthon, and the confessional documents presented by the other reformed groups were not even received. The Lutheran princes withdrew from the diet, and by midwinter they had formed a defensive alliance, the Schmalkaldic League, and the empire was split not only by religious differences but by political schism so deep and serious as to threaten almost universal European war. Within the year the Lutheran princes were being courted by Francis I for a new alliance against the emperor, in league with the pope and the Turkish sultan.

This sequence of events produced from Erasmus in Freiburg a last, long, agonized cry for concord. It was urged upon him by Julius Pflug, a German cleric, in the name of a considerable company of those who still shared Erasmus's hope for peace and who were still well disposed to him—some even in the imperial court. But Erasmus needed no urging: his cry came from the heart. The *Liber de Sarcienda ecclesiae Concordia* (On Mending the Peace of the Church) appeared from the Froben press in the summer of 1533, and it was quickly reprinted in Antwerp, Leipzig, and Paris.[7]

He had chosen the vehicle of a commentary on the Eighty-Third Psalm (84th) because of its appeal for a "beautiful and holy unity within the Church." This is always a profitable message "but especially does it appear of importance in this vicious age of sects, as it has in no other age" (331). The dedication of the psalm to the sons of Korah leads him to ruminate upon the sinfulness of that Old Testament figure and upon those who would visit the sins of the father upon his children, in contrast to the loving forgiveness of God who "does not impute our sins to us once we have repented of them" (338–39). But, he recalls, the sons of Korah did not repent. They attempted instead to divide the tabernacle ". . . as heretics and schismatics have always tried to rend the Church. Just as the wrath of God destroyed them, so for those who will not be warned to return to reason and abandon their impious sects and seditious attempts there remains the fire of hell" (339).

"Heretics insist they are the champions of the true religion [and] attempt to show that adherents to the Catholic faith are but tyrants and enemies of the Church. . . . Each heresiarch cries out that Christ is here, not there" (340).

But the church endures in its incomparable majesty despite them. It is true, he observes, that the church, like every other institution, is flawed by the insatiable nature of human desires, by abuses, and wicked practices, but such practices are no more a reflection of true Christian behavior than the equally execrable conduct of the sectaries. Let us all advance in faith "which works by love, practice justice, not of the law but of the Gospel, attributing to God all that we seem to do rightly" (357). For God wishes a unity of good men in His house "which is the Church." "If we wish to be blessed, let us with one voice praise God as the angels praise Him; in them there is no dissension" (361).

Unlike the angels, however, we must live and strive to praise God not in heaven but in the world, "a dark valley," true, "but a dark valley full of opportunities for being born, giving birth, dying, being sick and needy, sailing, waging war, and a thousand other tears" (365). It is a kind of exile from the Heavenly Jerusalem but not a bad place, on the whole. "There is no reason to dislike this valley," for its travails offer us the chance to keep God's faith and his commandments and thus "contrive to return to our homeland" (365). And above all—one of Erasmus's central themes—"the mercy of God is there, ready to lift us up in our infirmity and aid us in the path to perfection" (373).

The true church is secure from Catholic abuses as it is from Protestant attack, for it is "founded on the rock of Christ." The hope lies in all of us reforming ourselves, turning to Christ again who will transform disturbance into tranquility, with our help. Let popes act as true vicars of Christ; let rulers act as the divine justice directs; let magistrates fulfil their civil duties with good faith. Monks ought to exemplify the moral perfection to which their vows dedicate them; priests ought to meditate upon the law of the Lord. And let the laity keep their individual places and curb private hatreds and ambitions.

But what of the issues that divide the church so bitterly? He reviews them.

On the "thorny question" of free will Erasmus claims that

. . . we can at least agree that, of his own power, man can do nothing and is wholly dependent on the grace of God, in virtue of which we are what we are, so that in all things we recognize our weakness and glorify the mercy of God. (379)

The concept of divine mercy, after all, had always been more important to Erasmus than the questions of human merit or operative grace.

On justification by faith,

We must all agree in acknowledging the importance of faith. . . . let us agree that we are justified by faith, i.e. the hearts of the faithful are thereby purified, provided we admit that the works of charity are necessary for salvation. (379)

On the matter of saints and images, of feast days and dietary regulations—matters on which he himself had written so trenchantly—he now counsels compassion and tolerance. The "superstition" so widespread in the invocation of the saints should indeed be corrected:

Yet we must tolerate the pious simplicity of some, even when there is a certain amount of error involved. If our prayers are not heard by the saints, Christ, who loves simple souls, will give us what we request through the saints. . . . Those who rage against the images of saints have perhaps done so with reason, but to my way of thinking they have been a bit immoderate. Idolatry is certainly a terrible sin [but] statuary and painting have a place among the liberal arts as a kind of silent poetry. They occasionally catch the emotional state of man better than the eloquence of words. (380)

Feast days should not be abolished but their number should be reduced to those with some basis in Scripture. Fasting and dietary regulations should be interpreted sensibly and compassionately.

On the matter of confession, Erasmus agreed that at least "it is something that is salutary and useful to many and has the approval of many centuries of practice" (381). More than this will have to be decided by a council of the church.

As to the mass, Erasmus claimed that "wherever there is superstition and corruption it should be reasonably corrected. I see no reason why the Mass itself should be suppressed" (382). "There is no need that the Mass, accepted for so many centuries, should be stamped out like some impiety or pestilence" (383). On the related question of the cup to the laity which had, like every aspect of the mass, been so troublesome and divisive in the various reformed sects, Erasmus points out that this and like questions are merely external features, that in participating in the service it is "the communion that vivifies, and it does so without the sharing of the elements" (384). This is what we ought to emphasize and not the formal elements that divide us so bitterly.

The *De Sarcienda ecclesiae Concordia*, more than any of his other later works, tends to become a recapitulation of his religious philosophy.

These are its leading elements.

The old church, for all its faults, must remain the vessel of salvation, cleansed of its faults and abuses and opened to those who have fallen away. Religious unity—or religious peace if unity cannot be regained—is more important than the issues that divide men. On these issues themselves, both his enemies and some friends accused him of being willing to sacrifice essentials of religion for the hope of religious peace, and some modern scholars have subscribed to the same view. But the real essentials of Erasmus's religion remained, as strongly held in the *De Sarcienda ecclesiae Concordia* as so many years before in the *Enchiridion*—Christlike behavior, the Philosophy of Christ; disregard for the externalities of religion in favor of its substance; more confidence in the mercy of God than in his justice; and the passion for peace and brotherhood among Christians as the truest symbol of the imitation of Christ.

Even as he finished the *De Sarcienda ecclesiae Concordia* in a final rush to have it available for the Frankfort book fair, Erasmus was complaining again of having felt feeble all summer and that his strength had not yet returned. His always fragile health was failing. The excruciating attacks of kidney stone were more frequent and exhausting. Since the winter of 1530 he had endured a large stone in the bladder and feared it was only a matter of time until he suffered a fatal blockage. He was not yet willing to submit to the lithotomy widely (and often successfully) performed by contemporary physicians. "I will submit to surgery," he wrote, "only when I'm tired of living."[8] Arthritis added to his pain: he could not even sign his own letters in the last few years of his life and a firm handshake made him cry out in agony. He was further weakened by what were probably the after-effects of a mild contagion of the plague from which he never fully recovered. He was nervous and irritable, more restless and short-tempered than usual, his *famuli* complained.

He had always found it hard to forgive those who attacked him. In 1530 he had written a blistering open letter to the Franciscans, provoked by his quarrel with Carvajal—*Epistola ad quosdam impudentissimos graculos*—"supremely impudent nit-wits!"[9] In 1533, in another letter, he characterized his critics as "an endless throng of spiders and wasps, countless battalions of frogs and magpies, heaps of grasshoppers, and swarms of starlings and jackdaws. And even if these creatures did not have stings and beaks and claws, they could with their chattering alone drive a man out of his mind."[10]

In the spring of 1535 his friend Boniface Amerbach entreated him to return to Basel. Oecolampadius had now been dead almost four years and the canons of reform were somewhat relaxed, enough so that Amerbach could not only enjoy again the full citizenship of his city but enter once more into its councils. He had just been appointed rector of the university in the hope of reviving it. Surely he sought Erasmus's advice on that score. In any event, in May, he went in person to Freiburg to escort his old friend back "home," in a paneled wagon, to the house whose hospitality he had so often enjoyed, *Zum Luft*, Froben's house, where a room had been especially prepared for him.

Erasmus had taken a moment's uncharitable joy at the news of Oecolampadius's death as of Zwingli's in the same year, who was killed in battle at Kappel, fighting for his version of the reform. Stunica, Alberto Pio, Dorp were all dead. Luther was still alive, however, as were Bucer, Capito, Farel, Lee, Bedier, Carvajal, and Aleander. But it did seem that Erasmus was about to outlive his enemies. He had also outlived most of his friends, indeed most of his generation. Ammonio had died in 1517, Colet and Vitrier in 1519, Johann Froben in 1527, Wilhelm Kopp in 1532, his great English patrons Warham and Mountjoy respectively in 1532 and 1534, his old and faithful friend Peter Gillis of Antwerp in 1533. Then from England came word of the executions of Bishop Fisher and of Thomas More, the dearest friend of all his years. "There are tides of all human things," Erasmus wrote, "I myself seem to have died in More."[11]

These words were written on August 31, 1535. Erasmus's own end came within the year, on July 11 or 12, 1536. For a month he had been bedridden with dysentery. A few days before he died Boniface

Amerbach, with Jerome Froben and Nicholas Bischoff—who had taken over the Froben press—visited him and were so somber that he accused them of being the comforters of Job and asked cheerfully why they weren't tearing their clothes and heaping ashes on their heads. His last words were reported by Beatus Rhenanus, who had already taken over the task of completing his edition of Origen. "O Iesu, misericordia," he cried. "Domine libera me; Domine fac finem; Domine miserere mei," and finally, in the native Dutch which we have no record of his using for half a century, "Liever Got."[12] Perhaps at the end, as he had written in the *De Sarcienda ecclesiae Concordia*, Erasmus came "into the sight of Him who knows the secret places of the human heart."

Notes and References

Chapter One

1. The definitive edition of the letters is the *Opus Epistolarum Des. Erasmi Roterodami*, ed. P. S. Allen and continued by H. M. Allen and H. W. Garrod, 12 vols. (Oxford: Clarendon, 1906–1958), hereafter cited as EE.

2. *Ibid.*, I, 36–37.

3. *The Epistles of Erasmus from his Earliest Letters to his Fifty-First Year*, ed. and trans. Francis M. Nichols, 3 vols. (New York: Russell and Russell, 1962; originally published London: Longmans, Green and Co., 1901–18), I, 5, hereafter cited as Nichols. For the Latin see EE, V, Ep. 1437, p. 431. He even headed the letter with a Greek phrase, "To be read alone and in private."

4. Nichols, I, 5; EE, I, II, 47.

5. This is his phrase, again in Greek, from EE, V, Ep. 1437; rendered by Nichols, I, 5. He continues, ". . . nihil enim unquam me natum est infelicius. Sed fortasse futuri sunt qui multa affingent." Thus he also felt that unhappy as his early life had been, detractors might make it even worse if he himself did not supply his own account.

6. Most scholars now incline to follow the arguments of A. C. F. Koch, *The Year of Erasmus' Birth*, tr. E. Franco (Utrecht: Haentjins Dekker, and Gumbert, 1969), that 1467 was probably the correct year, in opposition to the arguments of E. W. Kohls, "Das Geburtsjahr des Erasmus," *Theologische Zeitschrift* (Basel) XXII (1966), 95–121, for the year 1466 and those of R. R. Post, "Gebootejaar en opleiding van Erasmus," *Mededelingen der Koninklijke Nederlandse Akademie* XVI (1953), 327 and "La Naissance d'Erasme," *Bibliothèque d'Humanisme et Renaissance* XXVI (1964), 489–501, for the year 1469. Koch's correlation of the known facts with external, datable events is persuasive. Less persuasive is his suggestion that apprehension over the approach of several climacteric years, as he grew older, made Erasmus shift his own statements about his birth year. Given Erasmus's contempt for astrology this seems unlikely. It may be possible, however, that some intimate of Erasmus, or even Erasmus himself, supplied the correct date to contemporary astrologers, interested in the horoscope of the great man. The best reason for Erasmus's evasiveness about his exact birth date remains his attempt to "back

date" it to a point before his father took holy orders. That this was, unfortunately, not the case, is implied in Leo X's brief of dispensation in 1517. See EE, II, Ep. 517, p. 434. Erasmus may well have misrepresented the facts in his negotiations for an earlier dispensation from Julius II, *ibid.*, III, Ep. 187ᴬ, xxix.

7. Nichols, I, 7; EE, I, 48.

8. The basic authority on the Brethren is Albert Hyma, especially in his *The 'Devotio Moderna' or Christian Renaissance* (Grand Rapids: The Reformed Press, 1924) and in relation to Erasmus, *The Youth of Erasmus* (Ann Arbor: Michigan, 1930). R. R. Post, in a more recent work, *The Modern Devotion* (Leiden: Brill, 1969) raises some important questions about the conventional view of the Brethren and their influence on Erasmus.

9. Nichols, I, 7; EE, I, 48.

10. Nichols, I, 8; EE, I, 49. This matter is mentioned also in the "Letter to Grunnius," Nichols, II, 343–44; EE, II, Ep. 447, p. 296.

11. *Ibid.*, Erasmus calls them *plagiarii*, "kidnappers."

12. Nichols, I, 9, *Compendium Vitae*; EE, I, ii, 49–50. The reference to his "betrayal" by his brother occurs just before this passage.

The same sentiment is expressed in "The Letter to Grunnius," Nichols, II, 351; EE, II, Ep. 447, 300–1. In that same letter he is even more bitter, calling him a Judas and adding, "Would that he had hanged himself like his prototype, before he had been guilty of so impious a crime," Nichols, II, 348; EE, II, Ep. 447, 298.

13. Nichols, II, 353; EE, II, Ep. 447, 301.

14. Nichols, I, 64; EE, I, Ep. 20, 99.

15. Nichols, I, 66–67; EE, I, Ep. 23, 105–7.

16. In the biographical letter of Beatus Rhenanus to Herman of Wied, Archbishop of Cologne in 1536, shortly after Erasmus's death and as a preface to an edition of Origen. Nichols, I, 23; EE, I, 55.

17. The reference to his memorizing Horace is contained in Beatus Rhenanus's parallel biographical sketch of 1540, written to Charles V as a preface to the first Erasmus *Opera Omnia*, Nichols, I, 36; EE, I, 70.

18. Nichols, I, 75; EE, I, Ep. 22, 103.

19. For this series see Nichols, I, 44–52; EE, I, Epp. 4–9, 77–87 and Appendix III. C. Reedijk, *The Poems of Erasmus* (Leiden: Brill, 1956), pp. 143–52, associates a number of his early poems with the same theme.

20. There is considerable controversy over both the date of composition and the sincerity of sentiment of this piece. See, for example, Paul Maestwerdt, *Die Anfänge des Erasmus* (Leipzig: Haupt, 1917), pp. 215–37 or John J. Mangan, *The Life, Character and Influence of Desiderius Erasmus of Rotterdam* (New York: Macmillan, 1927), I, 40, but especially Hyma, *Youth of Erasmus*, pp. 167–81. Bainton, *Erasmus of Christendom*, pp. 13–17, argues persuasively for the thesis that the work is an exercise. Albert Rabil, Jr., *Erasmus and the New Testament: the Mind of a Christian Humanist* (San Antonio: Trinity

University Press, 1972), pp. 18 ff, argues that Erasmus's shift to Christian Humanism is marked by the emphasis on Christian values and Christian sources even in this early work. For the prefatory letter to the eventual printed edition of 1521 see EE, IV, Ep. 1194, 457–58 as well as Allen's bibliographic matter in the introduction to the letter. The work itself is found in the standard *Opera Omnia Erasmi*, ed. J. LeClerc, 10 vols. (Leiden: Petrus Vander Aa, 1703–6), hereafter cited as LB.

21. Nichols, I, 20; EE, I, 2. See also Reedijk, pp. 49 ff.

22. Nichols, I, 75; EE, I, Ep. 22, 102–3.

23. From the prefatory letter to the printed edition of 1520, as translated in Hyma, *Youth of Erasmus*, p. 186. See EE, IV, Ep. 1110, 278, and I, 121, n. 16 for the history of the MS. The text itself has been definitively edited by K. Kumaniecki for the new Amsterdam *Opera Omnia*, vol. I (Amsterdam: North Holland Publishing Co., 1969), hereafter cited as *Op. Om. Amst.*

24. Nichols, I, Ep. 110, 225–26; EE, I, Ep. 118, 273–74.

25. Nichols, I, Ep. 122, 255–56; EE, I, Ep. 119, 274 ff.

26. Nichols, I, Ep. 122, 255–56; EE, I, Ep. 119, 274 ff.

27. Nichols, I, Ep. 112, 233; EE, I, Ep. 123, 284–85.

28. Nichols, I, Ep. 132, 283; EE, I, Ep. 138, 320 ff.

29. Nichols, I, Ep. 139, 300; EE, I, Ep. 139, 325–26.

30. Nichols, I, Ep. 168, 352–53; EE, I, Ep. 172, 380–81.

31. Nichols, I, Ep. 180, 374 ff; EE, I, Ep. 181, 403 ff.

32. Nichols, I, Ep. 132, 283; EE, I, Ep. 138, 321, n. 39, and Epp. 245, 270.

33. *Ibid.*, Ep. 185, 414–15.

34. The dispensation is reproduced from Vatican archives in *ibid.*, III, Ep. 187A, xxix–xxx.

35. Quoted in R. W. Chambers, *Thomas More* (London: Cape, 1948), p. 97.

36. Nichols, I, Ep. 191, 406–7; EE, I, Ep. 191, 422–23.

37. Nichols, I, 408; EE, I, Ep. 192, 423–24, the beginning of June, 1506.

38. Nichols, I, 417; EE, I, 4. See the elaborate account and edition of this poem by Jean Claude Margolin, "Le *Chant alpestre* d'Erasme," *BHR* XXVII (1965), 37–80. The standard modern text is in Reedijk.

39. EE, I, Ep. 205, 435.

40. *The Adages of Erasmus, A Study with Translations* (Cambridge: University Press, 1964), pp. 104–5.

41. Both these quotations are translated in Nichols, I, p. 438.

42. Nichols, I, pp. 438, 446.

Chapter Two

1. EE, II, Ep. 337, 94.

2. The text used is *The Praise of Folly* by Desiderius Erasmus, tr. and ed. Leonard F. Dean (Chicago: Packard, 1946), p. 132.

3. J. Austin Gavin and Thomas M. Walsh, "The *Praise of Folly* in Context: *The Commentary of Girardus Listrius*," *Renaissance Quarterly* XXIV

(1971), 193–209, argue that the *Moria* was actually a new, or newly derived, rhetorical form to its first readers, the "paradoxical encomium," an ironic blend of *dulce* with *utile*, of *salus* with *festivitas*. Rosalie L. Colie, *Paradoxia Epidemica: The Renaissance Tradition of Paradox* (Princeton: University Press, 1966), pp. 15 ff takes a slightly longer view but ties the *Moria* to the tradition of Renaissance paradox, as does Walter Kaiser, *Praisers of Folly: Erasmus, Rabelais, Shakespeare* (Cambridge: Harvard, 1963), pp. 35 ff. The detailed rhetorical analysis of the *Moria*, however, is best presented by Hoyt H. Hudson in his edition and translation of *The Praise of Folly* (Princeton: University Press, 1941). The *Moria* was, of course, also related—though to what extent we still do not know—to the rich tradition of fool literature. Erasmus was at least aware of the Latin edition of Sebastian Brant's *Ship of Fools* (1497) and perhaps some of its forerunners. See Enid Welsford, *The Fool* (London: Faber and Faber, 1935).

4. Nichols, II, Ep. 304, 169; EE, II, Ep. 304, 12–13.

5. The translation is by L. F. Dean in the intro. to his edition of *The Praise of Folly*, p. 2; EE, II, Ep. 337, 93. This letter was intended not only for Dorp but for the many who shared his views and thus Erasmus's response became a critical essay so extensive and pertinent that it was usually printed along with the text in later editions of the *Moria*.

6. Clarence H. Miller, the editor of the *Moria* in the *Op. Om. Amst.*, has shown in an unpublished paper "'Addunt, mutant': Erasmus's Additions and Revisions in *The Praise of Folly*" (which he was kind enough to send me in MS), that Erasmus added several lengthy and significant passages to the Schürer edition of 1514, in particular those about theologians and monks in Folly's long account of her followers and "new citations and new arguments to Folly's daring attempt to show that Christianity as it is revealed in the Scriptures is ultimately based on foolishness" (9). He argues that the immense popularity of the *Moria* by 1514 led Erasmus to use it to disseminate his increasingly definite religious and reforming ideas. He regards as significant too that it was only after these additions that the work began to be most seriously attacked by religious conservatives.

7. For an account of the evidence for Erasmus's authorship see *The Julius exclusus of Erasmus*, ed. and intro. J. Kelley Sowards, tr. Paul Pascal (Bloomington: Indiana, 1968), intro. pp. 7–23. See also James K. McConica, "Erasmus and the 'Julius': A Humanist Reflects on the Church," *The Pursuit of Holiness in Late Medieval and Renaissance Religion*, ed. Charles Trinkaus and H. A. Oberman (Leiden: Brill, 1974), pp. 444–71.

8. EE, III, Ep. 622, 45.

9. *Ibid.*, II, Ep. 502, 420.

10. Gilbert Highet, *The Anatomy of Satire* (Princeton: University Press, 1962), p. 18.

11. The text used is the Pascal translation cited above, n. 7, p. 46.

12. The text used is *The Colloquies of Erasmus*, ed. and tr. Craig R. Thompson (Chicago: University Press, 1965), p. 557.

13. *Ibid.*, intro. p. xxx.
14. The text used is *Ciceronianus or A Dialogue on the Best Style of Speaking*, tr. Izora Scott, ed. and intro. Paul Monroe (New York: Columbia Teachers' College, 1908), p. 21.

Chapter Three

1. See pp. 65–67 above.
2. EE, I, pp. 19–20. See also Ep. 164, the dedication of the 1503 printed edition, dated at St. Omer, (Autumn) 1501; EE, III, Ep. 858, the preface to the Froben edition of 1518, and references to later eds. For the identification of Poppenruyter see *ibid.*, VI, Ep. 1556, 42 and n. but especially Otto Schottenloher, "Erasmus, Johann Poppenruyter und die Entstehung des Enchiridion militis christiani," *Archiv für Reformationsgeschichte* XLV (1954), 109–16.
3. The text used is *The Enchiridion of Erasmus*, tr. and ed. Raymond Himelick (Bloomington: Indiana, 1963), p. 37.
4. Twenty years later he wrote a joint biographical account of the two men in a letter to Jodocus Jonas, EE, IV, Ep. 1211, June 15, 1521, which is also virtually the only account of Vitrier, whose name may actually have been Voirier. For this identification see Andre Godin, "De Vitrier à Origène: Recherches sur la Patristique d'Erasme," *Colloquium Erasmianum* (Mons: Centre Universitaire de l'Etat, 1968) and Alain Derville, "Un Aspect du Problème de la Réforme religieuse à Saint-Omer au Début du Seizième Siècle: Jean Vitrier et les Religieuses de Sainte Marguerite (1500–1530), *Revue du Nord* XLII (1960), 207–39. See also p. 122 below and Peter G. Bietenholz, *History and Biography in the Work of Erasmus of Rotterdam*, "Travaux d'Humanisme et Renaissance," LXXXVII (Geneva: Droz, 1966).
5. This preoccupation with Pauline inwardness and spirituality leads into what is the most curious aspect of the *Enchiridion*, its strong Platonic cast. More obviously than any other part of the book this is at odds with its original purpose. It was surely the result, in large part, of Colet's influence, for he was a thoroughgoing Platonist, as was Vitrier who apparently introduced Erasmus to Origen and perhaps Augustine in the Christian Neoplatonic tradition. And Erasmus was himself reading Plato. Beginning with chapter 5 of the *Enchiridion* he develops the typical Platonic soul-teaching; in chapter 14 he develops the Platonic epistemology and cosmology; and in chapter 28 the Pico-esque theme of "The Nobility of Man." Fully as curious as the inclusion of this Platonic excursus in the *Enchiridion* is the fact that it was Erasmus's only serious flirtation with Platonism. The Pauline framework remained central to his theological thought, the Platonic did not. Erasmus's Platonism is the subject of a considerable bibliography reaching back at least to Ivan Pusino's article, "Der Einfluss Picos auf Erasmus," *Zeitschrift für Kirchengeschichte* XLVI (1927). More recently P. O. Kristeller has again raised the question of the direct influence of Italian Neoplatonism upon him, arguing

that Erasmus, though he cited several Platonic dialogues in Greek, probably also used Ficino's translation of the Plato corpus. He also contended that Erasmus later made firsthand contact with Ficino's Neoplatonism in Italy. See his "Erasmus from an Italian Perspective," *Renaissance Quarterly*, XXIII (1970). Most authorities, however, argue for a more remote connection, stressing the influence of Colet and, more recently, of Vitrier. Rabil, p. 21, n. 60, even sees the Platonic element showing up in the earlier *Antibarbari*, at least in tentative form. In this assertion he follows Ch. Béné, *Erasme et Saint Augustin, ou Influence de Saint Augustin sur l'Humanisme* (Geneva: Droz, 1969). John B. Payne also argues for an early, pervasive, and continuing Neoplatonic influence in Erasmus's theology, particularly in his conception of the contrast between flesh and spirit. See his "Toward the Hermeneutics of Erasmus," in *Scrinium Erasmianum*, ed. J. Coppens, II, 17 ff. The more usual view, however, is that Erasmus's commitment to Platonism was rather superficial, unlike Colet's and that its peak was in the *Enchiridion*. See Rudolf Padberg, *Personaler Humanismus: das Bildungsverständnis des Erasmus* (Paderborn: Schoeningh, 1964); Alfons Auer, *Die vollkommene Frömmigkeit eines Christen* (Düsseldorf: Patmos, 1954); E. W. Kohls, *Die Theologie des Erasmus*, 2 vols. (Basel: Reinhardt, 1966). The tie between Vitrier, the influence of Origen, and the Neoplatonic tradition is of considerable importance in explaining the Platonism in the *Enchiridion*. See Godin; Edgar Wind, "The Revival of Origen," *Studies in Art and Literature for Belle daCosta Greene*, ed. D. Miner (Princeton: University Press, 1954); and Denys Gorce, "La Patristique dans la réforme d'Erasme," *Festgabe Joseph Lortz*, vol. I, *Reformation Schicksal und Auftrag* (Baden-Baden: Grimm, 1958), pp. 233–76.

6. *Erasmus of Christendom*, p. 65.

7. EE, I, Ep. 138.

8. Nichols, I, Ep. 134, 289; EE, I, Ep. 141, 232.

9. Erasmus himself notes Valla's influence on him in this regard in several references in the later controversies arising out of his own editing of the Greek New Testament. See EE, V, Ep. 1347, 243; I, 14; II, Ep. 300, 4–5; Ep. 384, 182; LB, IX, 15C. There is some scholarly speculation on the extent of Valla's influence on Erasmus's biblical scholarship. See, for example, Preserved Smith, *Erasmus, A Study of his Life, Ideals, and Place in History* (New York: Harper, 1923), pp. 159, 162; E. Harris Harbison, *The Christian Scholar in the Age of the Reformation* (New York: Scribner's, 1956), pp. 76, 85; Margaret M. Phillips, *Erasmus and the Northern Renaissance* (New York: Macmillan, 1950), p. 75; Hyma, *Youth of Erasmus*, p. 344; and David Lawrence, "The Influence of Lorenzo Valla's *Notes on the New Testament* on Erasmus' Decision to Publish the Greek New Testament," M.A. Thesis, Wichita State University, 1970.

10. Nichols, II, Ep. 236, 47–49; EE, I, Ep. 245.

11. Thomson and Porter, p. 136; EE, I, Ep. 246.

12. Nichols, II, Ep. 275, 101–2; EE, I, Ep. 282.

13. He refers to having finished his collation in a letter to Colet in the summer of 1513, EE, I, Ep. 270. For the identification of the MSS used *ibid.*, II, Ep. 373, intro.

14. Translation in Thomson and Porter, p. 184; EE, I, Ep. 296.

15. Erasmus did continue to view Birckman with hostility and in 1523 took him as the model for shady business practice as "the dedicated liar" in his colloquy "Pseudocheus and Philetymus, The Dedicated Liar and the Man of Honor." See *The Colloquies*, ed. Thompson, pp. 133 ff. One should note also at this point the incredibly forgiving nature of Bade who remarks in a letter to Erasmus about the Froben edition of the works that had been intended for him "to my detriment." But, he adds, "if this is for your interest or honour, I shall cheerfully put up with it," Nichols, II, Ep. 335, 215; EE, II, Ep. 346.

16. Nichols, II, 240–43; EE, II, Ep. 389.

17. Nichols, II, Ep. 380, 245–47; EE, II, Ep. 394.

18. Nichols, II, Ep. 393, 252–53; EE, II, Ep. 407.

19. Nichols, II, Ep. 377, 240–43; EE, II, Ep. 389.

20. Nichols, II, Ep. 395, 254–55; EE, II, Ep. 409.

21. EE, II, Ep. 423.

22. Gorce, p. 238.

23. Mattew Spinka, *Advocates of Reform from Wyclif to Erasmus*, "The Library of Christian Classics," vol. XIV (Philadelphia: Westminster, 1953), p. 288. It seems clear that, from beginning to end, Erasmus's personal favorite among the Christian fathers was St. Jerome. Some recent scholarship has argued for a much greater influence of St. Augustine upon Erasmus's theological views than previously recognized. The leading authority is Ch. Béné. *op. cit.* He demonstrates persuasively that the *Enchiridion* shows the influence of Augustine, especially the *De Doctrina Christiana*. But he argues less persuasively for the continuing Augustinian influence in both Erasmus's exegesis and his theology. Robert Peters (ed.), *Desiderius Erasmus, Prefaces to the Fathers, The New Testament, On Study* (Menston: Scolar Press, 1970), intro. p. 9, notes "Erasmus' temperamental unsuitability for work on Augustine." He was offended by Augustine's dogmatism. In Erasmus's *De Ratione Concionande*, which he wrote only a year before his death, he compared the various church fathers, still finding Jerome "always pertinent," preferring Origen for the fullness and aptness of his theology, but still lukewarm toward Augustine.

24. Desiderius Erasmus, *Christian Humanism and the Reformation, Selected Writings*, ed. John C. Olin (New York: Harper, 1965), p. 43.

25. Translation in Bainton, *Erasmus of Christendom*, p. 147.

26. *Ibid.*, p. 144.

27. Translation in John J. Mangan, *Life, Character and Influence of Desiderius Erasmus of Rotterdam*, 2 vols. (New York: Macmillan, 1927), II, 7; EE, II, Ep. 373.

28. The text used is in *Christian Humanism and the Reformation*, ed. Olin, p. 96.

Chapter Four

1. EE, II, Ep. 335.
2. Translation in *Erasmus and his Age, Selected Letters of Desiderius Erasmus*, ed. Hans J. Hillerbrand (New York: Harper, 1970), p. 108; EE, II, Ep. 541.
3. *Ibid.*
4. EE, II, Ep. 304.
5. The text used is in *Christian Humanism and the Reformation*, Olin (ed.), p. 57.
6. Letter to Reuchlin, Nichols, II, p. 375; EE, II, Ep. 457.
7. EE, III, Ep. 872.
8. *Christian Humanism and the Reformation*, Olin (ed.), p. 136; EE, IV, Ep. 1033.
9. Letter to Justus Jonas, May 10, 1521. Translated in *Selected Letters*, Hillerbrand (ed.), p. 158; EE, IV, Ep. 1202.
10. EE, V, Ep. 1528.
11. Quoted in Smith, *Erasmus*, p. 174.
12. *Selected Letters*, Hillerbrand (ed.), pp. 152, 155 ff; EE, IV, Epp. 1153, 1162.
13. EE, IV, Ep. 1196.
14. Quoted in Bainton, *Erasmus of Christendom*, pp. 176–77.
15. *Selected Letters*, Hillerbrand (ed.), p. 170; EE, V, Ep. 1352.
16. EE, V, Ep. 1324.
17. EE, V, Ep. 1419.
18. *Luther's Works*, vol. 32, pp. 92–94.
19. Translation in *Luther's Works*, "Letters II," vol. 49, ed. Gottfried G. Krodel (Philadelphia: Muhlenberg Press, 1972), pp. 77–81; EE, V, Ep. 1443.
20. The text used is *Erasmus-Luther Discourse on Free Will*, ed. and tr. Ernst F. Winter, "Milestones of Thought in the History of Ideas" (New York: Ungar, 1961), p. 20.
21. *Luther's Works*, *The Bondage of the Will*, tr. Philip S. Watson and Benjamin Drewery, "Career of the Reformer III" (Philadelphia: Muhlenberg Press, 1972), p. 10, n. 14. This is the best and most recent edition of Luther's reply but, for the sake of convenience, references below are to the Winter text, cited above, n. 26, for Erasmus' *Diatribe*, and containing both works.

Chapter Five

1. See above, p. 25.
2. Nichols, II, 120 ff; EE, I, Ep. 288.
3. The text used is in Margaret Mann Phillips, *The "Adages" of Erasmus* (Cambridge: University Press, 1964), pp. 309–10.
4. R. H. Bainton has argued, first in his "The *Querela Pacis* of Erasmus, Classical and Christian Sources," *Archiv für Reformationsgeschichte* XLII

(1951), 32–47, and even more strongly in his *Erasmus of Christendom*, pp. 120, 124, that in all his antiwar writings "the most significant contribution of Erasmus was his attack upon the basic weakness of the just-war theory."

5. The text used is *Querela Pacis, The Complaint of Peace*, in *The Essential Erasmus*, ed. and tr. John P. Dolan (New York: Mentor, 1964), p. 177.

6. *The Better Part of Valor, More, Erasmus, Colet, and Vives on Humanism, War, and Peace, 1496–1535* (Seattle: Washington University Press, 1962), p. 277.

7. Thompson (ed.), *The Colloquies*, p. 390.

8. Phillips, *Adages*, p. 220. He had much earlier expressed essentially the same sentiment in a work, remarkably like the later *Institutio Principis Christiani*, a letter-essay addressed to the young Adolphus van Veere, the son of his old patroness, entitled *Epistola exhortatoria ad capessendam virtutem ad generosissimum puerum Adolphum principem Veriensem*, written between 1498 and 1500 and printed by Martens in 1503 in the *Lucubratiunculae*. See EE, I, Ep. 93. Much later, in 1531, the same sentiment was expressed, "in him who is born to rule, virtue must from the outset be developed," as the guiding principle for a collection of classical quotations, not unlike the more famous *Adagia*, but specifically directed to the instruction of princes and dedicated to the young Wilhelm van Cleve. See EE, IX, Ep. 2431, the dedicatory epistle. The quoted passage was translated by Born (p. 9) from LB, IV, cols. 87–88.

9. It may have been started somewhat earlier, in 1515. The dedicatory epistle, EE, II, Ep. 393, is dated in March, 1516, after Erasmus's appointment as councillor in January. See also *ibid.*, I, 19 and II, 161, n. 205–8.

10. EE, I, 19.

11. Desiderius Erasmus, *The Education of a Christian Prince*, tr. and ed. Lester K. Born (New York: Norton, 1968), originally published 1936, p. 30.

12. EE, I, 19.

Chapter Six

1. Nichols, II, pp. 235–36; EE, II, Ep. 364.

2. Bietenholz, p. 45. Wallace K. Ferguson, *Erasmi Opuscula, A Supplement to the Opera Omnia* (The Hague: Nijhoff, 1933), p. 129, calls it "a new departure in the field of Christian biography." See also John B. Maguire, "Erasmus' Biographical Masterpiece: *Hieronymi Stridonensis Vita*," Renaissance Quarterly, XXVI (1973).

3. EE, IV, Ep. 999.

4. EE, IV, Ep. 1211.

5. EE, XI, Ep. 3037.

6. EE, VII, Ep. 1885.

7. The text used is in *The Essential Erasmus*, Dolan (ed.), pp. 327–88.

8. EE, VIII, Ep. 2263.

9. EE, VIII, Ep. 2275.

10. *Selected Letters*, Hillerbrand (ed.), p. 280; EE, X, Ep. 2892.

11. EE, XI, Ep. 3049.
12. EE, I, 53–54. He had, on occasion, made reference to Dutch proverbs, as to those in other vernaculars. As recently as 1531 he had quoted a Dutch proverb in writing to another Dutchman, his former *famulus* Hilary Bertholf, and again to his friend the Antwerp banker Erasmus Schets in 1533. See *ibid.*, IX, Ep. 2581 and X, Ep. 2781.

Selected Bibliography

BIBLIOGRAPHIES

There is an enormous volume of work on Erasmus. The following are the most useful guides to it. The standard bibliography for the early editions of Erasmus's own works is Ferdinand van der Haeghen, *Bibliotheca Erasmiana. Repertoire des Oeuvres d' Erasme*, 1st. and 2d. series (Ghent: Bibliothèque de l'Université de l'Etat, 1893). The most complete guides to the recent secondary literature are two successive volumes by Jean-Claude Margolin, *Douze Années de Bibliographie érasmienne, 1950–1961* (Paris: J. Vrin, 1963) and *Quatorze Années de la Bibliographie érasmienne, 1936–1949* (Paris: J. Vrin, 1968). See also the useful "Bibliographia Erasmiana," in *Scrinium Erasmianum. Mèlanges historiques publiés sous le Patronage de l'Université de Louvain à l'occasion du cinquième centenaire de la Naissance d'Erasme.* ed. J. Coppens, 2 vols. (Leiden: Brill, 1969), II, 620 ff. Useful also are two large cumulative bibliographies, the *Studies in Philology* "Annual Bibliography of Literature on the Renaissance," to 1970 and *Bibliographie Internationale de l'Humanisme et de la Renaissance* (Geneva: Droz. Annual since 1965). Both are elaborately indexed and contain nearly complete entries on every aspect of Erasmian scholarship.

ERASMUS'S WORKS

Following the catalogue prescribed by Erasmus himself, the Froben Press, immediately after his death, began work on the Erasmus *Opera*, probably supervised by his faithful friend Beatus Rhenanus. By 1540 the nine volumes of this work were published. His many editions of classical and patristic texts were omitted for reasons of economy, but it was otherwise as complete as possible.

By the end of the seventeenth century the Froben edition had become rare and expensive and another was undertaken by Petrus vander Aa, a Leiden bookseller, under the supervision of Jean Leclerc. It began to be published between 1699 and 1703, the entire ten volumes completed in 1707. The volume of letters was considerably increased over the 1540 edition and some apparatus was added, though unevenly. This has been the standard edition and will have to remain so until the completion of a superb new edition now being published.

This new edition is *Opera Omnia Desiderii Erasmi Roterodami, recognita et adnotatione critica instructa notisque illustrata.* Amsterdam: North-Holland Publishing Co., 1969—. The first volume has appeared in two heavy half-volumes, each item edited by an Erasmian authority, with Latin text and apparatus in English and French. The whole project is under the supervision of a distinguished international editorial board, chaired by Professor Cornelis Reedijk. Unlike either of its predecessors, this edition is massively edited.

Another equally massive project is also now under way, an English translation, *The Collected Works of Erasmus*, also a cooperative editorial work of many Erasmus scholars, being done by the University of Toronto Press. The correspondence volumes, under the editorship of D. F. S. Thomson and Sir Roger Mynors, are now being published and the volumes of the works will appear over the next several years. The University of Toronto Press also publishes a house organ of the project (since 1970), which contains not only progress reports but many useful notices and "tools" of Erasmus scholarship, *Erasmus in English.*

The standard edition of Erasmus's poetry is Cornelis Reedijk, *The Collected Poems of Erasmus* (Leiden: Brill, 1956). The items omitted from the Leclerc edition were collected in *Opuscula Erasmi, A Supplement to the Opera Omnia,* ed. Wallace K. Ferguson (The Hague: Nijhoff, 1933).

The standard edition of the correspondence remains the great *Opus Epistolarum Des. Erasmi Roterodami,* ed. P. S. Allen, and continued by H. M. Allen and H. W. Garrod, 12 vols. (Oxford: Clarendon, 1906–1958). The old standard translation, though partial and incomplete, is *The Epistles of Erasmus from his Earliest Letters to his Fifty-First Year,* ed. and tr. Francis M. Nichols, 3 vols. (London: Longmans, Green and Co., 1901–1918). A modern French translation is also being done, based entirely on the Allen edition, *La Correspondence d'Erasme,* ed. Alois Gerlo and Paul Foriers. Brussels and Quebec: Presses académiques européenes and Les Presses de l'Université Laval. Vol. I edited by Marie Delcourt appeared in 1967 and vol. IV, edited by M. A. Nauwelaerts, in 1970. Though restricted in scope see also *Erasmus in Cambridge: The Cambridge Letters of Erasmus,* tr. D. F. S. Thomson, intro. and commentary H. C. Porter. Toronto: University of Toronto Press, 1963.

For translations of individual works the reader is directed to the Notes and References in this book for those cited. He may also consult the bibliographies noted above.

WORKS ABOUT ERASMUS

1. *General Biographies*

Of the older biographies the most comprehensive is John J. Mangan, *The Life, Character and Influence of Desiderius Erasmus of Rotterdam,* 2 vols. (New York: Macmillan, 1927), but it is extremely hostile. Johan Huizinga, *Erasmus and the Age of Reformation*, tr. F. Hopman. (New York: Harper, 1957, originally published 1924); and Preserved Smith, *Erasmus, A Study of His Life, Ideals and Place in History* (New York: Dover, 1962, originally published 1923) both remain useful. The best biography yet is Roland H. Bainton, *Erasmus of Christendom* (New York: Scribner, 1969). Margaret Mann Phillips, *Erasmus and the Northern Renaissance* (New York: Macmillan, 1950), though slighter is also excellent, as is James D. Tracy, *Erasmus, the Growth of a Mind*, "Travaux d'Humanisme et Renaissance," vol. CXXVI (Geneva: Droz, 1972). Louis Bouyer, *Autour d'Erasme* (Paris: Cerf, 1955), is a sympathetic Catholic interpretation. *Erasmus*, ed. T. A. Dorey (London: Routledge and Kegan Paul, 1970), is a series of essays on aspects of Erasmus's life and work by eminent authorities.

2. *Special Topics*

a. *Aspects of his Life*

BIERLAIRE, FRANZ. *La Familia d' Érasme*. Paris: J. Vrin, 1968.

BRABANT, H. "Érasme, ses Maladies et ses Médecins." *Colloquia Erasmiana Turonensia, Douzième stage international d'études humanistes*, ed. Jean-Claude Margolin. Tours, 1969.

GEANOKOPLOS, DENO J. *Greek Scholars in Venice*. Cambridge: Harvard, 1962.

GIESE, RACHEL. "Erasmus' Knowledge and Estimate of the Vernacular Languages." *Romanic Review* XXVIII (1937), 3–18.

HOYOUX, JEAN. "Les Moyens d'Existence d'Erasme." *Bibliothèque d'Humanisme et Renaissance* V (1944), 7–59.

OELRICH, K. H. *Der Späte Erasmus und die Reformation*. Münster: Aschendorff, 1961.

THOMPSON, CRAIG R. "Erasmus and Tudor England." *Actes du Congres Erasme, Rotterdam 27–29 Octobre 1969*. Amsterdam and London: North-Holland Publishing Co., 1971.

———, "Erasmus as Internationalist and Cosmopolitan." *Archiv für Reformationsgeschichte* XLVI (1955), 191–95.

b. *Aspects of his Work*

BAINTON, ROLAND H. "The Paraphrases of Erasmus." *Archiv für Reformationsgeschichte* LVII (1966), 67–75.

BOUYER, LOUIS. "Erasmus in Relation to the Medieval Biblical Tradition." *The Cambridge History of the Bible*, ed. G. W. H. Lampe. Cambridge: Cambridge University Press, 1969. II, 492–505.

BRACHIN, PIERRE. "Vox clamantis in deserto: Réflexions sur le pacifisme d'Érasme." *Colloquia Erasmiana Turonensia*. I, 247–71.

COPPENS, J. C. L. "Les idées réformistes d'Érasme dans les Préfaces aux Paraphrases du Nouveau Testament." *Analecta Lovaniensa Biblica et Orientalia*. Louvain, 1961. Ser. III, fas. 27.

FERGUSON, WALLACE K. "Renaissance Tendencies in the Religious Thought of Erasmus." *Journal of the History of Ideas* XV (1954), 499–508.

GORCE, DENYS. "La Patristique dans la Réforme d'Érasme." *Festgabe Joseph Lortz.* Vol. I. *Reformation Schicksal und Auftrag.* Baden-Baden: Grimm, 1958.

HADOT, JEAN. "Le Nouveau Testament d'Erasme." *Colloquim Erasmianum.* Mons, 1968.

HALKIN, LÉON E. *Erasme et l'humanisme chrétien.* Paris, 1969.

JARROTT, C. A. L. "Erasmus' Biblical Humanism." *Studies in the Renaissance* XVII (1970), 119–52.

KOHLS, ERNST-WILHELM. *Die Theologie des Erasmus.* Basel: Reinhardt, 1966.

MARGOLIN, JEAN-CLAUDE. "L'Idée de Nature dans la Pensée d'Erasme." *Recherches Erasmiennes,* "Travaux d'Humanisme et Renaissance," CV. Geneva: Droz, 1969.

MESNARD, PIERRE. "La *Paraclesis* d'Érasme." *Bibliothèque d'Humanisme et Renaissance* XII (1951), 26–42.

PANOFSKY, ERWIN. "Erasmus and the Visual Arts." *Journal of the Warburg and Courtauld Institutes* XXXII (1969), 200–27.

PAYNE, JOHN B. *Erasmus: His Theology of the Sacraments.* Richmond: John Knox Press, 1970.

———. "Toward the Hermeneutics of Erasmus." *Scrinium Erasmianum.* II, 13–49.

RABIL, ALBERT, JR. *Erasmus and the New Testament: The Mind of a Christian Humanist.* San Antonio: Trinity University Press, 1972.

SCHNEIDER, ELIZABETH. *Das Bild der Frau im Werk des Erasmus von Rotterdam.* Basel: Helbing und Lichtenhahn, 1955.

Index